CONTENTS

INTRODUCTION   PAGE   8

MIGRATIONS AND BATTLES   PAGE   22

A TWIN CAPITAL   PAGE   52

MEMORIES OF AN EMPIRE   PAGE   82

STEPPES AND VINEYARDS   PAGE   112

THE COLORS OF LIFE   PAGE   126

INDEX   PAGE   134

Hungary
PLACES AND HISTORY

Text by Claudia Sugliano

1 The equestrian statue of St. Stephen, the first Catholic king of Hungary, stands near a tower in the Fishermen's Bastion.

2-7 This view of fortified Buda probably dates to 1612, the period in which Hungary was mostly Ottoman.

3-6 Almost fairy-tale in appearance, the Bridge of Chains is shown against the background of the river and the castle that rings Buda hill.

Graphic design
Cristina Cassaro

Editorial coordination
Federica Romagnoli

Translation
Timothy Stroud

ISBN 88-8095-751-1

Color separation: Grafotitoli
Bassoli srl, Sesto S. Giovanni (MI)

*I*f a survey were held in western Europe on Hungary, almost certainly, most people would be able to name Budapest as its capital; over the centuries, famous visitors to the city have called it 'the pearl of Europe', 'as lovely a river view as London on the Thames or Paris on the Seine', 'a dream city' and 'the queen of the Danube'.

The 'disproportionate head' of a small state measuring just 36,000 square miles and with a population of 10 million people, Budapest has always had the ambitions of a capital of a vast kingdom. It has its own fascination that, in the collective imagination, almost overshadows its rather uniform nation, however, considering the history of Hungary, its capital has always been 'peripatetic', as the following cities have all held that honor at some time: Székesfehérvàr (the Roman city of Alba Regia), Pozsony (today Bratislava) and even Vienna. The kings of Hungary lived and were buried in the first, the legislative assembly used to meet in the second and the Hapsburgs dominated the entire region of the rivers Danube and Tisza from the third.

The territory of the country has also undergone large changes over the centuries: three seas have bathed its borders at one time or another, but invasions, wars and peace treaties have 'amputated' entire regions from its body, and later perhaps reattached them, each time to form a new political entity.

What has marked this fiery, combat-ive people has been their capacity to survive despite the catastrophes and invasions they have suffered, to maintain their sense of identity intact and to preserve their musical language, Magyar (an idiom that originated in ancient Asia) in the midst of the deluge of German, Latin and Slav languages that engulfed them.

For some, the heart of Hungary is Lake Balaton, a vast freshwater inland sea that appears, on the map, to be the country's point of reference. This important water basin, the largest one in Central Europe, does not lie exactly at the center of the country but many Hungarians consider that it is around it that the nation revolves.

Lake Balaton is the epitome of the country, with its variety of landscapes and styles of architecture and the almost marine sense of freedom given by this vast and placid body of water–though it is sometimes marked by dramatic storms.

8 top left An extraordinary view of the large river and its wooded surroundings is seen from Viségrad, the heart of the Danube Bend and the ancient royal residence of Hungary.

8 top right The large Sumeg Castle in the quiet town of Transdanubia was built in the thirteenth century by the bishops of Veszprém but fell into abandon in 1700 following a fire.

8-9 The riverbank in Pest, on the left side of the Danube, is lined with palaces from the early 1900s. The political, economic and cultural center of the capital, this part of the city stretches into the plain.

9 bottom A column raised in 1763 by the Association of Serb Merchants as an offering for having survived the plague stands in the main square of Szentendre, on the Danube Bend.

10 top Veszprém Castle stands solidly on a rocky spur in the center of the city among the hills of the Bakony forest to the north of Lake Balaton. A cultural center in the region, the city was the seat of the first Hungarian episcopate and where the bishop had the privilege of crowning the queens.

10 bottom Breeding sheep for their wool is common in Hungary, especially in the Great Plain. Here a flock near Kalocsà puts up with the winter cold as it searches for grass in the bleak, snowy landscape.

10-11 The land between the Bodrog and Tisza rivers enjoys exceptionally fertile soil and a warmer, sunnier climate than the rest of the country. Laid out like a geometric design, these are the vineyards that produce the grapes for Tokay wine, named after the region.

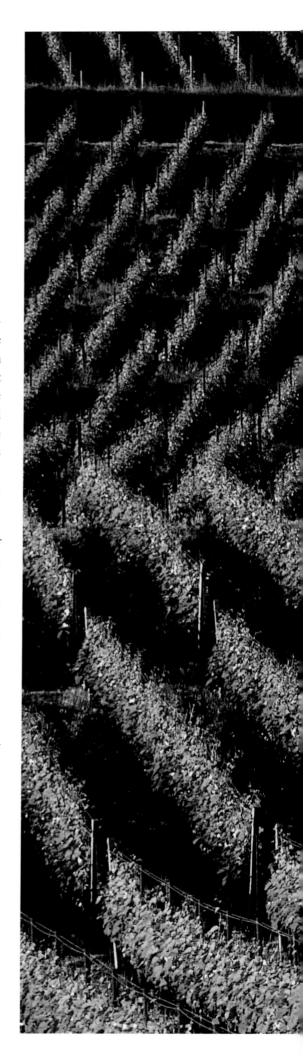

Water is one of the motifs of a nation whose landscape is devoid of particular features. It has the Great Plain with its puszta where herds of horses and flocks of sheep roam; then there is the majestic Danube and the more whimsical Tisza, innumerable streams and thermal waters and spas that have been known and used since Roman times (this is mirrored in the name Aquincum, which was chosen for the regional capital of Pannonia, now a district of Budapest).

The landscape is not mountainous, but rolls gently over low hills, some-

times volcanic in origin, which are often covered in vineyards; and some zones enjoy an almost Mediterranean climate. The basins of the two largest rivers in the country, with their fertile soil suitable for agriculture, attracted the Magyars, who arrived from the Urals. Here the Asian nomads settled as farmers, creating the basis for an economy that is still one of Hungary's main resources.

The cultivation of the land and the long-established farming traditions of the people provide the thread that runs through the history of the country. It has been a disputed history, featuring invasions, destruction, revolts and internal conflicts that have destroyed many of this small nation's architectural monuments, defensive strongholds and large castles and restricting its urban culture to limited zones. For example, King Stephen I, the king-saint who, around 1000, founded the country of Hungary, was obliged to fight rebellions against the feudal system he had introduced shortly after converting to Christianity and being crowned with the crown sent to him by Pope Sylvester II.

In the thirteenth century, the Mongol invasion brought new ruination and, in 1526, the Turks conquered the country and ruled it for the following 150 years. The central area of Hungary, dominated by the Ottomans, still contains a few minarets, mosques and domed public baths as relics of that dark era.

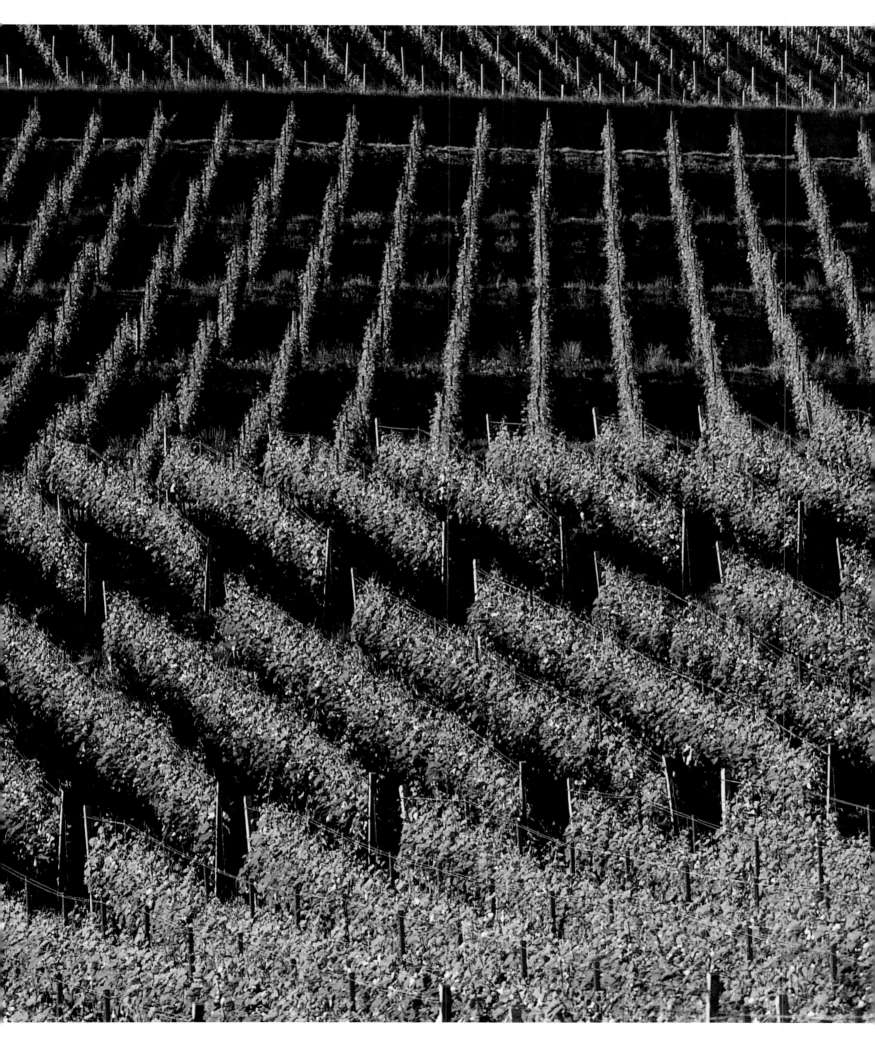

The remaining forts in Hungary were destroyed by the Austrians to prevent insurrections against their 'liberating' troops and to prevent the union with the Hapsburgs.

Although there are more ruins than monuments from the past, the farming culture is the form that best represents the past of the country. It is imbued with ancient values and has a folklore that is one of the richest in Europe: including, for example, the uràlàs, a dance-cum-spectacle performed at New

Year by the Csàngòs people in the village of Egyhàzaskeszo (the Csàngòs are a Magyar minority that emigrated from Rumanian Moldavia during the war), the fearsome, grotesque devils of Mohàcs and the poetic Easter ceremonies in Hollòkò.

To discover Hungary, the visitor must explore its unpretentious lifestyle that has remained unaltered in its quality and simplicity. It is as though the past is harmoniously integrated in the life and landscape of the villages and cities of today, such as Sopron, Pécs, Szeged,

Kecskemét or Debrecen. In all of these places it is possible to admire the mosaic created by history, architecture and art, aided by the easy contact with the Hungarian people who have not forgotten the ancient duty and pleasure of offering hospitality.

And for those wishing to feel the pulse of twenty-first-century Hungary, there is its capital, which in 1585 had enchanted Ambrogio Calepino. 'Three of Europe's cities are pearls: Venice, on the water, Buda, on the hills, and Florence, on the plain', wrote the Italian encyclopedist, and who would contradict him today as one admires the cohesion of hilly Buda, with its castle and Mount Gellert crowned by the citadel, and the plain of Pest, covered by a cobweb of streets and alleys overlooked by domes, spires and Art Deco towers. Though it has suffered great destruction over the centuries, this 'Paris of the East', as it has been called for its lively atmosphere and enjoyment of life, has always risen from the rubble both architecturally and culturally and maintained a specific role for itself in Europe. It is as though Budapest, living through the chiaroscuro of its history, had learned that it could continue to heal its wounds, renew itself and grow without erasing its past. Improving the view of this large urban agglomerate spread over hill and plain, there is the greenery of the parks and Margaret Island and also, more importantly, the silver ribbon of the Danube with which Budapest lives in extraordinary symbiosis.

25 bottom Istvan I (King Stephen) was crowned on 1 January 1001 and is considered the founder of the Magyar state and the defender of the Roman Church. He was canonized in 1081 for having preserved the autonomy of the country. Stephen was the founder of a patrimonial monarchy based on the possessions of the king and was also responsible for the progressive restructuring of society by partially redistributing wealth and creating a new division of labor.

Following the devastating Mongol invasion of Hungary (1241-42), the second founder of the country was Bela IV (1235-70). After having annihilated the Magyar army at Muhi, the Golden Horde demolished the fortifications in Pest in just three days, and the survivors took refuge in the hills of Buda, just across the Danube. But the river froze over and allowed the invaders to cross, where they took possession of Buda and destroyed it before continuing west. Shortly after, inexplicably, the Mongol leader, Batu Khan, turned around and headed back to Asia, but Hungary was already devastated and fell prey to famine. Returning from exile, Bela IV dedicated himself to the enormous task of rebuilding the state and giving it a modern foundation. One of his priorities was the construction of a chain of fortified cities as these had been the only ones able to resist the Mongol raids, and this strategy led to the construction of the defensive wall of Pest-Buda. Churches, houses and ecclesiastical chancelleries were also built; Buda rapidly grew with gothic buildings laid over the ruins of the Romanesque ones. At the end of Bela's reign, Buda was a flourishing city, as it was to remain until the tragic invasion by the Ottomans in 1541. With the death of Andrew III in 1301, the Arpad dynasty died out resulting in the Hapsburgs and the Neapolitan branch of the Angevins advancing rights to the crown of Saint Stephen on the basis of marriages between their families and a number of Hungarian princesses. After an eventful struggle between various candidates to the throne, Charles Robert of Anjou (1308-1342) won out and became the first of a series of foreigners to rule the country. Although the new king made Buda the capital and called a Diet in Pest in its honor, he preferred to live first in Temesvàr (Timisoara, now in Rumania) and then in the gothic palace in Visegràd. This was where he called a central European summit in 1335 at which the kings of

26 This battle scene is taken from the Cronica Hungariae and shows Bela IV, the Hungarian king (1235-70) facing up to the troops of Otakar, the Bohemian king.

Poland, Czechia and Hungary agreed an alliance, prevalently economic. Rather than conducting wars of conquest, Charles Robert dedicated himself to defeating local powerful oligarchs; another achievement was the agreement he reached with the burghers of Buda, reconfirming the ancient freedoms of the city and thereby enriching its inhabitants once more. The Angevin king also modernized the army and the administration and reformed the monetary and banking systems and, under his rule, Pest-Buda became the largest trading center in central Europe, even though it was almost a century late in its urbanization compared to other important cities in the region. Charles Robert's son, Louis I the Great (1342-82),

inherited a peaceful and prosperous country but immediately initiated a policy of international aggrandizement with the aim of taking Hungary up to the level of Europe's major powers. However, his wars in Italy and the Balkans weakened the Magyar kingdom, even as the Ottoman threat was growing. Louis I, however, showed himself to be a great political and administrative reformer; one of his most important acts was the convocation of a Diet in Buda from which a revision of the Golden Bull was issued in 1351 that regulated the privileges of the nobles and was to remain in force until 1848. One of the privileges allowed the nobles to direct public affairs, which was another way of saying they could enter politics.

26-27 The two panels in the altarpiece of St. Lambrecht church, painted by Hans von Tuebingen (1430) and conserved in Graz Landesmuseum, are dedicated to the victory won by Louis I against the Bulgars. The king was the son of Charles Robert of Anjou and wanted to raise Hungary to the level of a European state through wars of conquest. This won him the nickname 'Louis the Great'.

Louis died without a male heir and so was succeeded by his daughter Maria, who ceded the throne on her death to her husband, Sigismund of Luxemburg (1387-1437), who became the most powerful sovereign in Europe when he was elected German king in 1411 and became titular king of Bohemia in 1419. It was he who inspired the Council of Constance that

condemned Jan Hus and therefore put an end to the schism based on religious reformation (1414-18) and who organized summits in Buda with European kings. With the Ottomans still pressing, Sigismund organized a crusade against the Turks but was defeated at Nicopolis, and thus it was that his successor, Albert Hapsburg (1437-39), decided to entrust the defense of the southern border of the

28 top right King Sigismund I – Holy Roman Emperor and King of Bohemia – distinguished himself for the brutality he used in putting down the Hussite rebellion. The revolt had originated in Bohemia and tried to spread into Hungary by taking advantage of the miserable conditions of the peasants. This incunabulum from 1488 by Johan de Thwrocz – kept in the Biblioteca Marciana in Venice – shows an episode from the war against the followers of Jan Hus conducted by a coalition of Saxons, Szekels (a tribe from the Carpathians) and Hungarian nobles.

28 bottom left Albert II Hapsburg, king of Germany from 1438-39, allied himself with emperor Sigismund against the Hussites and married Sigismund's daughter. He succeeded the emperor in 1438 on the thrones of Bohemia and Hungary but died in 1439 before being crowned emperor.

28-29 The battle of Nicopolis (1326) is depicted here in a painting held in the National Library in Paris. We see the Turkish victory over the Hungarian troops led by Sigismund. Following this success, the Ottomans undertook further forays into Hungarian territory. In 1456, however, they were beaten by Jànos Hunyadi near Belgrade, thereby destroying the Turkish bridgehead into Hungary. In 1476, Matthias Corvinus defeated the invaders once more but, following the death of Mahomet II, the Turks succeeded in taking Hungary.

country to Jànos Hunyadi, who was a rich landowner in Transylvania. Hunyadi served two monarchs, Vlaszlo I Jagiellon (1440-44) and the boy king Ladislas V Hapsburg the Posthumous (1453-57). The life of this general was in practice dedicated to the struggle against the Turks, in which he had alternating fortunes. The battle of Varna (1444) was a heavy defeat, in the course of which Ladislas I died, but, in 1456, Hunyadi recorded a great victory over Mehmed II at Nàndorfehérvàr (Belgrade), which not only saved Hungary but also Europe from the Ottoman threat for the next 70 years.

29 right The fifteenth-century Chronicle of Ulric di Richental illustrates the court of Sigismund of Luxemburg and Maria, eldest daughter of Louis the Great and queen of Hungary and Poland. At the age of two, Maria was betrothed to the youngest son of the Czech king and emperor, Charles IV, who was later educated at the Hungarian court.

30-31 *Engraved by the Parisian Gèrard Jollin between 1670 and 1700, this lovely view of fortified Buda, with the castle and church spires, bears the definition of the city as 'the loveliest and strongest in Hungary and also its capital, situated on the Danube, one of the largest rivers in Europe, which crosses this kingdom'.*

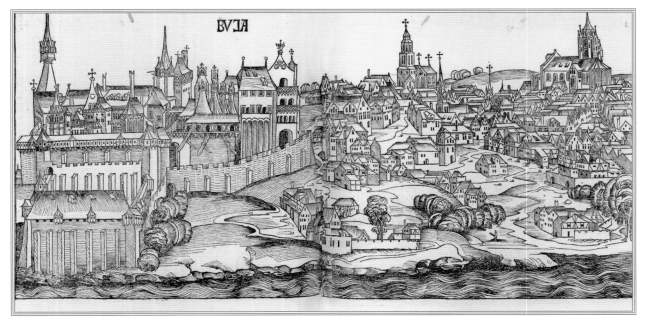

30 bottom *Hartmann Schedel's 1493 woodcut shows south Buda as it was around 1470. At the left, there is the royal palace, which was enlarged and made more comfortable by the cultural patron Matthias Corvinus to accommodate scientists, intellectuals, artists and their works. The design was by Cimenti Camicia and the work by Dalmatian and Italian craftsmen. The main court was enlarged and hanging gardens based on those in Urbino were created.*

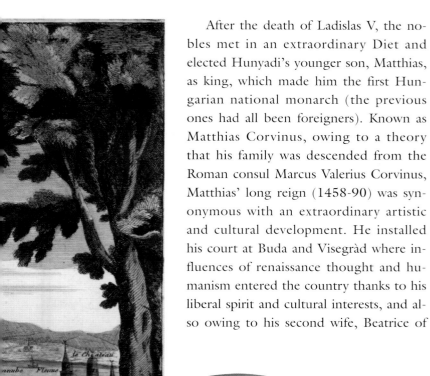

After the death of Ladislas V, the nobles met in an extraordinary Diet and elected Hunyadi's younger son, Matthias, as king, which made him the first Hungarian national monarch (the previous ones had all been foreigners). Known as Matthias Corvinus, owing to a theory that his family was descended from the Roman consul Marcus Valerius Corvinus, Matthias' long reign (1458-90) was synonymous with an extraordinary artistic and cultural development. He installed his court at Buda and Visegràd where influences of renaissance thought and humanism entered the country thanks to his liberal spirit and cultural interests, and also owing to his second wife, Beatrice of Aragon, of Italian origin. Matthias I was the initiator of contemporary Magyar culture and became the symbol of the nation; this role is still recognized today, and monuments dedicated to him can be seen in symbolic locations such as the Buda hills, in front of the Danube, and in the square of Cluj-Napoca cathedral. Unfortunately, this sovereign, who fought with the Church against the Hussites and who conquered Bohemia, Moravia and Slesia, did not have a worthy successor. Vlaszlo II Jagiellon (1490-1516), who was already the Czech and Polish king, was elevated to the throne with the support of the oligarchs but was always in their thrall.

31 left Beatrice of Aragon, the daughter of the king of Naples, was Matthias Corvinus' second wife. An important dynastic association, their marriage brought the influence of the Italian Renaissance to the Hungarian court.

31 right Matthias Corvinus, portrayed here in ivory by the Lombard school (1485-90), defeated the Turks and inaugurated a period of prosperity for Hungary.

REGINA HVNGARIÆ
BEATRIX DE ARAGONIA

REX
MATHIAS HVNGARIÆ

In 1514, a peasant uprising broke out led by Gy'orgy Dòzsa, and in 1521, the Turkish leader, Suleiman the Magnificent, led his troops westward into Hungarian territory, which fell easily to him. One of the cities he took was Nàndorfehérvàr, where Jànos Hunyadi had previously defeated the Turks. The situation worsened quickly for the Hungarians, who had neglected their fortresses and let their standing army disband. They were unable to find support from other states; for example, Sigismund of Poland signed a peace treaty with Suleiman. On 29 August 1526, the battle of Mohàcs between the pitiful Hungarian forces under Louis II Jagiellon (1516-26) and the Suleiman's Turkish army ended in a rout and the death of Louis. In September, Suleiman entered Buda without resistance to find the capital almost deserted. One of the consequences of the defeat at Mohàcs – the worst in Hungarian history – was the splitting of the kingdom into three parts: the central and southern regions ended up under Ottoman domination, the less important northern and western area became part of the Hapsburg empire and Transylvania in the east was transformed into an autonomous principality under Turkish suzerainty and later became the center of the fight for national independence. The Ottomans did not contribute much to the country, limiting themselves to the construction of a few public baths and mosques. Hungary's well-structured Christian society

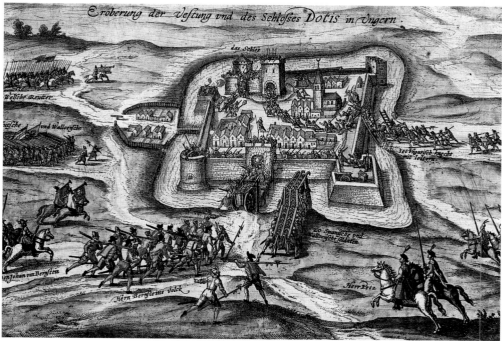

was not easily assimilated and put up strong resistance to the Ottoman dominance. In 1571, the Holy League led by the Hapsburgs was able to report a victory over the country's occupiers, but it was only in 1686 that Buda was liberated from Turkish dominion after the imperial army had occupied Transylvania. The following year, the Pozsony Diet renounced the right to elect the king and recognized the eternal right of the Hapsburgs to the Hungarian throne. In 1699, the Peace of Karlowitz marked the end of Turkish occupation of the country.

Taking advantage of the role it had played in the chasing out of the Turks, the Hapsburgs considered all the lands won back as theirs by right, which provoked a people's rebellion. Eighty years earlier, the resistance against the Hapsburgs had been concentrated mostly in Transylvania where Istvàn Bocskai had succeeded in winning independence from Vienna in 1605-06, in which one of his demands was free religious worship for Protestants. In 1703, another uprising occurred under the powerful landowner and prince of Transylvania, Ferenc II Ràkòczi, but after a struggle lasting eight fruitless years, he was forced to accept a compromise with the Austrians. The reigns of Maria Theresa (1740-80) and Joseph II (1780-90) were brushed by the Enlightenment and introduced some measure of reform, creating a degree of collaboration with the Hungarian nobility, but the absolute power of the sovereign was re-established under Francis I (1792-1835), the emperor of Germany and king of Bohemia and Hungary. Three Diets met between 1825 and 1839, ushering in an era of reforms in which Istvàn Széchenyj played an important role. The Diet of 1839 freed political prisoners and allowed the middle classes to own land and exercise administrative functions. The revolution that broke out in France in 1848 had repercussions in Hungary and, on 15 March, the people rose in Pest under the guidance of Kossuth and the poet Sàndor Petofi, sparking off a nationwide revolt for reform and independence. The struggle was inconclusive for over a year, but once the Austrian army (supported by the Russians) had retaken Pest and Buda, the Hungarians were obliged to lay down their arms.

35 top This famous engraving is held in Vienna city museum and shows the young queen, Maria Theresa (1740-80), with her newborn son (the future Josef II) in her arms as the nobility swear to sacrifice 'their lives and their blood' to save the throne from their Prussian rival. At the beginning of Maria Theresa's reign, the nobles supported the new queen with enthusiasm though conflict became inevitable owing to their refusal to give up their feudal rights.

However, weakened by defeats in Italy and Prussia, the Austrians signed a compromise with Hungary in 1867 in which an Austro-Hungarian state was created. The Hungarians had the right to a separate government but the ministries of defense, foreign affairs and finance remained in common with the Austrian ones. The emperor, Franz Josef I, thus became king of Hungary. Despite the people's opposition to the agreement, the economy of the country began to improve and Budapest began to take on the appearance of the great city that we know today. Catastrophe arrived in 1914 with the plunge into the First World War of the Austro-Hungarian monarchy in alliance with the Prussian empire, which led to enormous loss of life. On Franz Josef's death, his successor, Charles I, became the last ruler of the Hapsburg Empire with his coronation in the Matthias church on 30 December 1916. Aware of the weakness of his army, Charles unsuccessfully attempted to negotiate a separate peace with the Allies; with the war coming to an end, a democratic-bourgeois revolution headed by Mihàly Kàrolyi broke out that resulted in the abdication of the emperor and the proclamation of the republic in 1918. Three years later, Charles I twice attempted to return to the Hungarian throne but he was opposed by the ruling Magyar class and died the following year in Madeira. A democrat and a liberal, Kàroly became president of the republic and divided the land between the peasants, but the enormous social and economic problems led to a union between Communists and Social Democrats who together took power under the aegis of the new Communist party. For 133 days, Béla Kun headed a Republic of Soviets, in a period marked by fierce repression.

36 bottom Due to internal hostility in Bohemia and Hungary, and following defeat on the Italian front, Franz Josef was obliged to cede something. In 1867 he recognized a limited form of Hungarian independence but financial, military and foreign policies remained common responsibilities.

37 top In 1906, Franz Josef I (1830-1916) was present at the inauguration of the equestrian monument dedicated to Stephen I, the king-saint and founder of the Magyar state. It was erected in Buda by Lajos Stròbl in front of the Fishermen's Bastion.

37 center Charles IV (1916-18) succeeded Franz Josef to the Austrian throne and was crowned king of Hungary in 1917. He attempted to conclude a separate peace with the Entente Cordiale and proposed a series of liberal reforms and concessions to national minorities, but his efforts were in vain.

37 bottom On 16 November 1918, the Republic of Hungary was proclaimed. The end of the monarchy had been heralded since the end of the summer when a National Council, led by the liberal democrat Mihàly Kàrolyi, had asked for a separate peace with the Entente Cordiale, Hungarian independence, recognition of the rights of minorities, land reform and universal suffrage. On 31 October, the crowd took to the streets and Archduke Josef, nominated homo regius by the king, appointed Kàrolyi Prime Minister.

38-39 On 21 March 1919, an immense crowd celebrated the new Hungarian government of Soviets, which was initially well received owing to the rapid taking of power by the Communist, the support of the middle class intellectuals and the disillusionment and disorientation of the masses who sympathized with and trusted Kun.

This was a people's demonstration on April 1950, during the Communist regime, that celebrated the anniversary of the Communist Liberation of the country. The demonstrators filed past the portraits of the Soviet leaders, Vladimir Lenin and Joseph Stalin, which hung beside that of the head of the Hungarian government, Matyas Ràkosi (center).

45 top After Stalin's death in 1953, the moderate Communist, Imre Nagy (center), succeeded Matyas Ràkosi. Though he had decided to put right the regime's most evident wrongs, he was unable to remain in power as he was opposed by the Soviet Union.

45 center The steel mill in Sztalinvarosz (today Dunaùjvaros) was the flagship of Communist industry in Hungary. The steel plants in Ganz and Weiss were nationalized in 1946, but the bauxite mines and aluminum industry survived two more years.

45 bottom With the ratification of the new Constitution on 20 August 1949, the era of Matyas Ràkosi (secretary of the Hungarian Communist party) began the period of Stalinist rule in the country. When Horthy had been in power, Ràkosi spent a long period in Moscow, whose directives he followed blindly. After Imre Nagy's brief mandate, he returned to govern the country in 1955.

The republic was proclaimed on 1 February 1946, with Zoltàn Tildy as president, and a year later the Treaty of Paris was signed with the Allies, which returned Hungary's borders to how they had been in 1938. During new elections in 1947, which were forced owing to a worsening economic situation, the Communist party was elected and the country became part of the Soviet bloc. The struggle of the church against the regime led to the arrest of the country's Primate, Cardinal Jòzsef Mindszenty, and to his life imprisonment for plotting against the state. The Stalinist phase of Hungarian history began under Màtyàs Ràkosi with many executions, including that of the minister Làzslò Rajk. After Stalin's death a period of fluctuation began, and the Prime Minister, Ràkosi, was deposed in favor of the Communist reformer Imre Nagy. Two years later, however, Nagy was expelled from the party.

46-47 A student
demonstration on 23
October 1956 turned
into an uprising that
forced the government
to resign. Ernö Gerö,
who had replaced
Ràkosi, ordered
military repression
and a revolution
broke out across the
country. The symbols
of Communist power
were torn down and
on 24 October even the
gigantic statue of
Stalin, in Budapest's
György Dósza
Boulevard, was
knocked over, dragged
through the streets and
smashed to pieces.

46 bottom October
1956. Budapest was the
theater of bitter
fighting, with the rebels
even supported by some
soldiers. Many of these
were later sentenced to
death following the
intervention of
Russian troops,
when even General
Pàl Maléter joined
the revolt.

47 top right During the insurrection, portraits of Matyas Ràkosi, the secretary of the Hungarian Communist party, were burned in the streets. He was the hated symbol of the oppressive regime and the puppet of the Soviet Union.

47 left The protest extended to the whole country and focused on symbols of Communist power linked to the Soviet Union. Here soldiers remove Lenin's portrait from the Council Room in the Municipality of Gyor in western Hungary.

47 bottom right In October 1956, the crowd throngs a Budapest street trying to get hold of a copy of a newspaper that supported the uprising.

The revelations of Stalin's crimes by Nikita Khruschev at the 20th Congress of the Communist Party of the Soviet Union allowed a breath of fresh air to enter Hungary. On 23 October 1956, a simple peaceful demonstration led to the successful October Uprising, which demanded free elections, the freedom of the press and the departure of Soviet troops from the country. Imre Nagy returned to head the government, but only 11 days later, on 4 November, the Soviet army entered Hungary and in just two weeks re-established 'order' at the price of 25,000 lives. Deported to Rumania, Imre Nagy was sentenced to death two years later with his ministers.

48-49 *The Red Army bloodily put down the uprising in 1956. The clashes brought the deaths of 3,000 and wounded 13,000; 15,000 more were sentenced in various ways, including 300 executions. As a result, 200,000 people (2% of the population) chose exile.*

49 top left *People in Budapest examine destroyed military vehicles in Joszef Koerut Street. The buildings were damaged by Soviet artillery.*

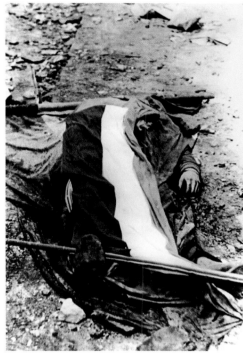

49 center left *National symbols took on enormous importance during the insurrection: here the body of a combatant is covered in an act of pity and pride by the Hungarian flag.*

49 bottom left *Another dramatic scene during the October 1956 revolt: bodies lie on a lorry flying the black flag; in the foreground, a soldier proudly wears a beret with the national symbol that replaced the red star.*

49 right *The revolt also cost heavy losses to the Soviets; here the body of a Russian soldier lies close to the remains of a troop vehicle. During those terrible days, the strength and courage of the 'small' Hungarian people caught the attention of the world.*

50 top Jànos Kàdar, the head of the government after the uprising, is shown on his return from New York where he had taken part in an assembly of the United Nations.

50 center In June 1989, the bodies of Nagy and his collaborators were given state burials and they were all rehabilitated a few months later.

50 bottom In March 1999, Hungary entered NATO after ten years as an independent and democratic republic. This photograph shows a meeting of foreign ministers held in Budapest in 2001.

50-51 The supreme body of power in Hungary, the Parliament, has 386 members who are elected for a period of four years. The 2002 elections returned a liberal-socialist coalition to power. Parliament also elects the president of the republic, whose term of office lasts five years.

The long era of Jànos Kàdàr from 1966-88 began with an authoritarian and repressive period rigidly aligned to Soviet foreign policy, but with the passing of the years, relaxation was gradually made and a small private sector and series of economic reforms came into being. The reforms of 1968 were insufficient, however, and a serious economic crisis arose in the 1980s. In 1988, Kàdàr was replaced and the following year brought important changes: the Assembly accepted the principle of transition towards a multiparty state on 16 June

with the official recognition of the nationwide insurrection in 1956. A state funeral was held for Imre Nagy followed by his political rehabilitation.

In May, the foreign ministers of Hungary and Austria symbolically cut the fences that separated the two countries and, in October, the National Assembly changed the name of the country from the People's Socialist Republic to the Republic of Hungary. Thanks to unstoppable changes caused by Gorbachev's perestroika, the Soviet Union had also changed direction. An agree-

ment between the two countries led to the withdrawal of the Soviet troops and the first free elections were held in 1990; shortly after, Hungary entered the European Council. The 1994 elections were won by the Socialist party, led by Gyula Horn, who succeeded in creating a coalition government. Since 1999, Hungary has also been a member of NATO, confirming the country's commitment to greater Europe, a characteristic that has distinguished it from the earliest days of its difficult but glorious history.

A TWIN CAPITAL

52-53 The suspension bridge Szabadád hid, or Liberty Bridge, was built in 1896. During Second World War many bridges in Budapest were damaged or destroyed, but this stunning work of engineering survived.

53 top The elegant baroque enclosure of the Castle can be entered via a number of stairways, from which picturesque views of the Danube, Mount Gellert and Pest are offered.

53 center The eclectic architecture of Budapest includes modern designs, such as this umbrella-shaped fountain in Blaha Square. The underpass always features groups of buskers.

53 bottom The Bridge of Chains connects Pest to Castle Hill. A tunnel runs under the hill and a neo-classical entrance designed by Adam Clark. The Scottish engineer saved the bridge in 1849 while it was under construction when he flooded the rooms that contained explosives before the retreating Austrian troops could blow it up.

52 top left Located in front of Liberty Bridge at a strategic point in Buda, one of the most important buildings in the district on the southern slopes of Mount Gellert is the complex of the Baths and the Hotel Gellert, characteristic of Hungarian Art Nouveau.

52 top right Pest is the lower city that lies on the plain on the left bank of the Danube and is the most cosmopolitan and modern part of the capital. Its architecture is typified by the eclecticism of its superb neo-gothic, neo-renaissance and classic imperial styles and by the buildings of the Secession period.

T he city of Budapest was created in 1873 when the three sister cities – and often rivals – of Pest, Buda and Obuda joined together. A tour of this, one of the most fascinating cities in Europe, must begin from Castle Hill in Buda, the district where the history of the city began. This elevation, about 200 feet above the Danube, has always been a lookout spot as it gives a superb view of the river and of Pest stretching away on the other bank. The stones used to construct buildings in the past tell of a tormented history in which Hungary tried tenaciously to maintain its own identity when oppressed by foreign occupying forces: first the Turks, then the Austrians. Despite its modest height, Castle Hill was of military importance before the invention of the cannon, when catapults were the principal means of defense against a besieging force. For that reason, King Béla IV moved his residence here in the thirteenth century from Obuda, on the plain that stretches alongside the Danube. According to the Austrian composer Johann Strauss, who dedicated one of his most famous waltzes to the Danube, the river changes character in Magyar territory, with its tranquil nature transformed until it almost 'skips with joy'. The royal residence was built on the south slope of the hill with the fortified city on the north side. Archaeological research has shown that the ancient city's topographical shape remained practically unaltered, despite sieges, wars and rebuilding during the Hungarian capital's history. Even today,

the outline remains the same after five hundred years. The heart of the district and the symbol of the country's most glorious era is the Matthias Church (Màtyàs-Templom). It is of uncertain origin but appears to have been first constructed in 1015, however, some sources claim that the first version was a Romanesque church built by Béla IV in the mid-thirteenth century. What is certain is that Charles Robert of Anjou was the first king to be crowned there in 1308, and that Sigismund of Luxemburg and the emperor of Byzantium attended a service here in 1424. Both the first and second marriages of Matthias Corvinus were cel-

ebrated in the church but during the Turkish occupation it was turned into a mosque. After being rebuilt by the Jesuits, it underwent extensive restoration between 1784 and 1896 and was used to crown two Hapsburgs, Franz Josef I in 1867 and Charles IV (the last king of Hungary) in 1916. Damage suffered during the Second World War when the German troops used it as a deposit was repaired over a period of 20 years after the war. The church is built in French gothic style and has a roof made from shiny, multicolored painted tiles. Its two towers flank the façade, one built by Béla and the other by Matthias, the latter being octagonal and topped by a spire. One en-

54 left Trinity Square in Buda is dominated by the thirteenth-century Church of Our Lady of the Assumption, better known as the Matthias Church, which is a symbol of the most glorious age of the country. The 250-foot-high church tower gives great views over the city. The church has been important in Hungary's history: this is where the coronation of Charles Robert in 1308 and the blessing of the standards before the wars with the Turks took place.

54 right The Matthias Church is in neo-gothic style with a few decorative elements harking from the Middle Ages, but it was actually built in the late 1800s. The panels dedicated to Saint Imre were painted by Mihàly Zichi, and the windows and frescoes were by Kàroly Lotz and Bertalan Székely. The statue of the Virgin stands in a large almond-shaped niche and is illuminated by golden light.

55 The main entrance is on the west side of the church and has a lovely nineteenth-century low relief by Lajos Lantai of the Madonna and Child with two angels. The portal on the south side, known as 'Mary's Door', is decorated with a superb gothic low relief of the 'Dormition of the Virgin', reconstructed by Frigyes Schulek in the early 1900s.

ters the church through the side door (Maria's Door, as the church is in fact dedicated to the Virgin though known by the name of Matthias) to the interior, which is adorned with standards. The pillars are painted green, ocher and yellow with the medieval ones decorated with paintings or Art Nouveau motifs. To the right of the main entrance, the Loretta Chapel has a superb statue of the Madonna that was offered by Ladislas II; to the left, the Trinity Chapel contains the funerary monument to Béla III (twelfth century) and his wife Anne of Chatillon. The neo-gothic high altar dates to 1800, and the crypt, where the church's treasure is held, contains a number of stone tombs and a marble sarcophagus dating to the Arpad dynasty.

The equestrian statue (1906) that stands in front of the south face of Matthias Church is by Alajos Stròbl and represents Saint Stephen, the first Christian king of Hungary and the founder of the state. In the center of the nearby Trinity Square (Szenthàromsàg tér) stands the ornate eighteenth-century Trinity column that was raised after the dreadful epidemic of the plague in 1712-14. The only modern building, the Hilton Hotel, stands over the site of a monastery marked by the statues of the monks Julianus and Gellért. The hotel combines ancient architectural

elements, such as the Roman milestone and a thirteenth-century cloister. Next to it is the turreted neo-Romanesque Fishermen's Bastion (Halàszbàstya, 1905), which was so named because it stands on the site of an ancient fish market, or perhaps as a tribute to the Guild of Fishermen whose duty it was to defend the city in the Middle Ages. The bastion has a long, patrol walkway that makes for a wonderful promenade giving incomparable views over the Danube and Pest. The Castle district is also the setting for Buda's ancient City Hall, a lovely eighteenth-century building in Italian baroque, with a turret and a clock. The spirit of the district is quickly appreciated when threading one's way through the many narrow streets that lie around Trinity Square, where old houses are decorated with frescoes and wrought ironwork.

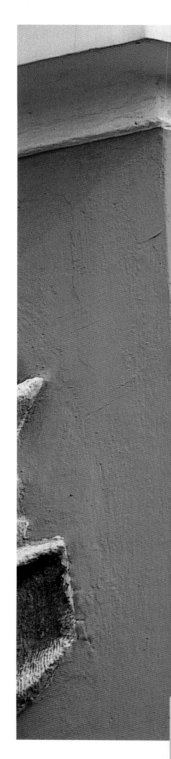

Fortune Street (Fortuna Utca) was once known as Frenchmen's Street because it was where French craftsmen invited by King Matthias once lived. The seemingly gothic eighteenth-century building at number 4 was once Frenchmen's Inn. Diet Street (Orszàghàz Utca) takes its name from the building at number 28, inspired by German baroque, where Buda's Parliament used to meet. At the center of a row of baroque houses, three gothic buildings (numbers 18, 20 and 22) stand out. Attractive squares lie in the midst of these small streets, like Andràs Hess Square (Hess Andràs tér) where there stands the twentieth-century statue of Pope Innocent XI, who supported the reconquest of the city from the Turks, and the eighteenth-century 'house of the red hedgehog' that is formed by the union of different medieval buildings. The Vienna Gate Square (Bécsi Kapu tér) is surrounded by baroque buildings but the brick square itself was built in 1923 and contains the National Archives. Capistrano Square (Kapisztràn tér) is named after the Italian monk who accompanied Jànos Hunyadi on his military campaigns; the solitary tower in the square belongs to the old Church of Saint Mary Magdalene, the only Christian temple that was left open in Buda during the Turkish domination. Tàrnok and Uri Streets (the latter, the 'Street of the Lords', is the longest in the Castle district) lead to Arms Square (Dìsz tér). Here, between the royal residence and the burghers' quarters, was where public executions took place and, in the Middle Ages, where the market was held.

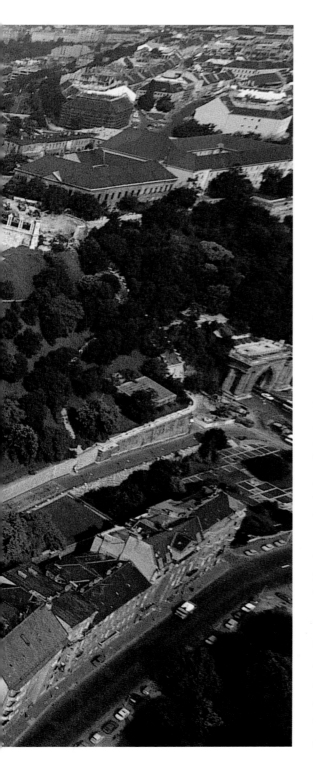

Saint George's Square (Szent Gyo'rgy tér), with the neo-gothic Sandor Palace and the rococo Fortress Theater, faces towards the main entrance to the Royal Castle (Kiràlyi Vàr); though its massive appearance is not very attractive, the gigantic palace has been internally restored to display the valuable museum collections. It was during the years after the Mongol invasion of Magyar territory in 1241 that King Béla IV decided to build a fort, then partly demolished in the fourteenth century by two Angevin kings with the intent to enlarge it. Sigismund of Luxemburg made several improvements and turned it into his residence, and the humanist king, Matthias Corvinus, had it redone in renaissance style. He had gardens laid out and installed the Corvinus Library which, at the time, was the most important in Europe. Though the castle did not suffer damage when it fell into the hands of the Turks in 1541, the siege of 1686 was heavily destructive, so Charles III had the first south wing built, and, during the reign of Maria Theresa, extensive rebuilding did away with the old sections of the castle. From 1791, the new building became a residence of a branch of the Hapsburgs, and further rebuilding between 1890 and 1905, in neo-baroque, was followed after the Second World War by heavy reconstruction after the castle was severely damaged. During this last rebuilding operation, remains of the medieval fortress were discovered. The entrance to the castle is marked by an attractive neo-baroque wrought iron gate on which the turul, the mythical bird and symbol of the Magyar tribe, is featured with a sword gripped in its talons. The 330-yard baroque façade of the castle overlooks the Danube and has at its center, below the large dome, the equestrian statue of Eugene of Savoy, one of the liberators of the city from the Turks. It is also possible to see the restored ancient fortifications, including Saint Stephen's Tower, Ferdinand Gate and the New World Gate. The largest defensive element of the complex, the south barbican, has walls over 16 feet thick. The northwest court features the twentieth-century bronze fountain of King Matthias hunting.

Of the museums in the palace, the Hungarian National Gallery (Magyar Nemzeti Galéria) is without doubt the most important with its collection of works by Hungarian artists from the Middle Ages to the present day. The late-gothic altarpieces, triptychs like 'The Angelus of Sibiu' and various polyptychs can be seen in the Old Throne Room. Magnificent sculptures include the 'Head of the King of Kalocsà', 'Saint Dorothy of Barka' (1410-20) and 'Saint Stephen of Mathéos' (1500-10). The best represented period is from 1800 to the early 1900s with several rooms dedicated to Mihàly Munkàcsy, a realist and one of the greatest Hungarian painters, Laszlo Paàl, a landscape artist from the Barbizon school, Kàroly Ferenczy, an impressionist and a master of plein air painting, and Jòzsef Rippl-Rònai, whose work was influenced by Art Nouveau and Japanese prints. The museum also has monumental works of historical subjects like the 'Baptism of Vajk' by Gyula Benczùr and 'Miklòs Zrìnyi at the battle of Szigetvàr' by Pèter Krafft. The Budapest Historical Museum (Budapesti To'rténeti Mùzeum) is in the east wing of the castle and recounts the history of the city from ancient times to the modern day through archaeological collections, jewelry and pottery. Some rooms have ogival ceilings and majolica stoves. There is also a small gothic chapel that was rediscovered in the 1960s. The National Library, founded in 1802 by Count Ferenc Széchény, contains 35 volumes from the original famous library belonging to Matthias Corvinus.

62 top left The red marble head of the king of Kalocsà is exhibited in the Hungarian National Gallery and is considered a masterpiece of Hungarian Romanesque. Only six inches high and by an unknown artist, the perfection of the proportions and skill in the modeling are superb.

62 top right The Budapest History Museum (Budàpesti Torteneti Mùzeum) is in the east wing of the Castle. It describes the history of Buda, Pest and Obuda, the three cities from whose union Budapest was created in 1873. It has a magnificent collection of gothic statues found in 1974.

62-63 'The refugees' by Sziney Merse Pal (1845-1920) hangs in the Hungarian National Gallery. Its realistic and pathos-filled style is typical of the artist whose early works include 'Breakfast on the grass' (1873), one of the first European masterpieces of plein air painting.

63 top right The Hungarian National Gallery (Magyar Nemzeti Galéria) is dedicated to Hungarian painting and sculpture from the Middle Ages to the twentieth century. The collections of the Lapidary Museum are restricted to the Middle Ages and the Renaissance.

63 center right The Hungarian National Gallery has many gothic polyptychs with gold grounds, some of which are exhibited in the former Throne Room.

63 bottom right This is a room of neo-classical sculpture in the Hungarian National Gallery. The museum offers fine views of the Castle.

64 Gerardo Gellert, one of the early Christian missionaries in Hungary, was from Venice. He died when he was thrown off the slopes of Mount Gellert (430 feet) into the Danube by Hungarian pagans. Now his statue overlooks that same panorama.

65 left The octagonal pool in the Turkish

Rudas Baths – one of the loveliest in the city and built for Sokoli Mustafa, the pasha of Buda from 1566 to 1577 – lies in a room topped by a spherical dome and adorned with glass tiles and eight columns.

65 top right At the foot of Mount Gellert, the Elizabeth Bridge crosses the river at a strategic point. On the opposite bank we see

the parish church in the city center, which was built in the twelfth century over the ruins of the Roman walls of Contra Aquincum.

65 bottom right Apart from their beauty, the bridges of Budapest are the links in a symbolic chain that joins the two banks and the two souls of the Hungarian capital.

A flight of steps leads from the Fishermen's Bastion down to Vìzivàros (the 'city of the waters'), which is the strip of land that runs between the hill and the river and where one of Buda's oldest districts stands. It contains remains of the Turkish dominion, like the Kiràly Baths.

Adam Clark Square is one of the nerve centers of the traffic that runs between Buda and Pest, and is named after the Scottish engineer who using Tierrey Clark's project, built the Bridge of Chains and the tunnel under Castle Hill in the nineteenth century.

The Fo' utca has some lovely baroque buildings and the ancient Capuchin monastery, with gates and windows in Ottoman style. Batthyàny Square is the location of the Church of Saint Anne, which is rich with artworks and one of the city's most interesting examples of baroque architecture.

Still on the Buda side of the river, close to Margaret Bridge are the thermal baths of the Upper City. They contain two traditional baths named Lukas' Bath and the Emperor's Bath; the latter is Turkish in origin but was rebuilt in neoclassical style. They are both fed by ten springs of calcareous and sulfurous water at temperatures between 63-149°F.

Erzsèbet Hìd is an elegant suspension bridge dedicated to the Empress Elizabeth (the famous Princess Sissy). It leads to Mount Gellert, which overlooks the Danube at its narrowest point, a distance from bank to bank of just 660 feet. It was from this hill that Saint Gellert (also known as Saint Gerardo), one of the evangelizers of Hungary, was thrown to his death into the river. His statue stands half hidden in the gardens.

An imposing Liberation Monument was erected to commemorate the liberation of Budapest in 1945 from the German troops. It stands on the top of the hill where the Austrians blockaded the Citadel for four years between 1850-54.

Before leaving the right bank, there is still Obuda to see, the district that was originally colonized by the Romans.

66 top The ruins of Aquincum reveal the layout of a flourishing Roman city with a grid of streets, a sewage system, thermal baths and a covered market.

66 bottom Fötér was built on the ruins of the Roman city and is one of the few eighteenth- or nineteenth-century districts remaining in Obuda (Old Buda).

66-67 Fötér, the principal square in Obuda, is the ideal backdrop for the bronze statues of figures holding umbrellas by Imre Varga.

The ruins of the city of Aquincum, which was founded 2,000 years ago and had a population close to 60,000 inhabitants, include an amphitheater, a large basilica and the villa of Hercules with mosaic floors. There is also a Roman museum. The entire district is tranquil, seemingly provincial, with alleys, gardens and brightly colored houses. There is the eighteenth-century Zichy palace, the Vasarely Museum, dedicated to Victor Vasarely (the founder of optical art, who emigrated to France in 1919 at the start of the Horthy dictatorship), and the Imre-Varga Museum, dedicated to two important twentieth-century Hungarian sculptors. They produced many public works, including the nearby bronze group of four women with umbrellas.

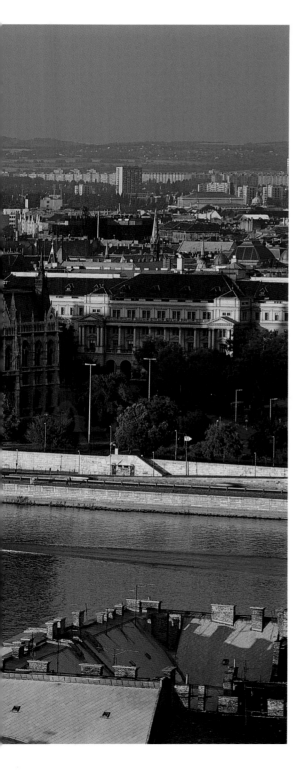

The flat left bank of the Danube is a world apart from the historic Buda. This is where Pest lies, a city of lovely nineteenth- and twentieth-century buildings that line broad avenues like those in Paris or Vienna. It is a district filled with life and shopping areas.

The large Lajos Kossuth Square is named after one of the country's leaders in the War of Independence (1848-49) and was one of the places where crowds gathered to cheer the proclamation of the Hungarian Republic on 23 October 1989. It is the setting for statues of Lajos Kossuth, Ferenc II Ràkòczi (another national hero) and Mihàly Kàrolyi and Imre Nagy (modern era politicians).

The square is looked down on by the Parliament, now the seat of the National Assembly, which is a majestic building designed by Imre Steindl in eclectic style. It mixes Byzantine, Venetian, Romanesque and gothic and has a dome 312 feet high. Inside, the main staircase and rooms are decorated with gilding and frescoes. Another building lining the square is the neo-renaissance Ethnographic Museum (the former Courthouse) on the pediment of which the goddess of Justice is carved.

An interesting example of secessionist architecture is at number 4, Hold Utca, just past Liberty Square (Szabadsàg tér), designed by the architect Odon Lechner. Lined with yellow majolica tiles and bricks like a flowery field, this building houses the National Bank of Hungary.

70 center right The imposing Saint Stephen's Basilica (1851-1906) by Miklòs Ybl is an excellent example of the neo-renaissance style this architect loved. The building is where the reliquary of Stephen's right hand is kept.

70 bottom right The Vigadò (The Lobby) in the square of the same name is a concert room built by Frigyes Feszl between 1850 and 1864 in an eclectic style of rare harmony. Sculptures of dancers on the columns flank portraits of kings and famous Hungarians.

71 This detail of the main entrance to the basilica dedicated to Saint Stephen shows the elegant clypeus representations of the twelve apostles.

70 left Gresham Palace is one of the most beautiful secession-style buildings in Budapest. Its curved lines and plant decorations are crowned by the bust of Sir Thomas Gresham, the founder of the Stock Market in London.

70 top right Before crossing the Bridge of Chains in 1867, Emperor Franz Josef took an oath then he went to go first to Buda Castle where he was to be crowned king of Hungary.

The nineteenth-century Basilica of Saint Stephen stands in the square of the same name. It resembles Saint Paul's cathedral in London and can hold 8,000 worshippers. Roosevelt tér, the square dedicated to the American President, looks towards the Bridge of Chains and is distinguished by two important buildings: the Gresham Palace (1907), in secessionist style, and the neo-renaissance Hungarian Academy of Science, which is adorned with allegorical statues.

In Pest's 'inner city' or 'citadel', i.e., the medieval city, there are many busy squares, such as Deàk Ferenc tér, with its Lutheran temple, and Szervita tér, whose Servite Church of Saint Anne is a lovely baroque design.

Another lively square is Vigado tér, which faces the Danube and has a superb view of Buda that is best enjoyed while seated in the sunshine at one of the many cafés.

The square has one of the city's most attractive theaters, the Pesti Vigadò, which is an extraordinary example of architectural and decorative excess in late nineteenth-century Hungarian styles. But the real center of this area of Pest is Vo'ro'smarty Square, dedicated to the great romantic poet Mihàly Vo'ro'smarty, whose white marble statue stands in the center of the piazza.

72 top The shops in Vaci Street offer a wide array of goods, especially Hungarian handcrafts like embroidery, fabrics, pottery, porcelain, paprika and the excellent barackpàlinka, a type of apricot brandy.

72 center The central market was built at the end of the nineteenth century by Samuel Petz with a lovely brick façade, portico, neo-gothic towers and a roof of shiny colored Zsolnay majolica tiles. The building was part of a project for five covered markets.

72 bottom The covered market has food products like fruit, vegetables, salami and cheeses on the ground floor. Souvenirs and Hungarian goods are for sale in the gallery that circles the building on the first floor.

The Gerbeaud patisserie was founded by a family of Swiss origin and is one of the city's favorites for its early 1900s atmosphere and delicious cakes. Vàci utca, the pedestrian area, is a busy shopping street so it is no surprise to find the Mercury fountain on the corner (besides being the messenger of the gods, Mercury was also the guardian deity of tradesmen). The road continues as far as Liberty Bridge (Szabadsàg hìd) where Budapest's central market is located in a fine brick building from the end of the nineteenth century, with neo-gothic towers, a roof covered with Zsolnay majolica tiles, porticoes and a large clock. The city's loveliest baroque monument, however, stands in University Square (Egyetem tér): it is the University Church, which was built between 1725-42 by Mayerhoffer and has magnificently carved wooden pews and a pulpit. Another baroque church is the Franciscan one built on the site of a former mosque. It was here that Franz Liszt retired to spend a period of quiet in a monastery and used to assist at the mass. Parallel to Vaci Street runs the small City Hall Street (Varoshàz utca), almost suffocated by the Hall itself, the largest building in old Pest. Maria Theresa used to say that this building was more beautiful than its Viennese equivalent, the Burg, with its three floors, long façade, two low reliefs depicting the military campaigns of Charles III and Eugene of Savoy and another relief by the famous artist Margit Kovàcs (1949).Avenues are typical of Pest, and Small Avenue (Kisko'rut) runs in a semi-circle from Liberty Bridge to Deàk Square along the line of the fortifications.

72-73 Gerbeaud patisserie is perhaps the most famous in Budapest. It was opened in 1858 but bought out by the Swiss who gave his name to it and redecorated the interior. Famous throughout central Europe, the patisserie was even visited by the Viennese to fill up with dry brioches and spicy pogàcsas.

73 top Vaci Utca is the central street in Budapest. It has many magnificent late nineteenth and early twentieth-century buildings but is first and foremost a shopping street. Progressively closed to traffic in the past years, now Vaci Usta is reserved to pedestrians only.

74 top Hungary's double crown was created in the twelfth century. The lower half (known as the 'Greek' part) has figures of saints and Greek inscriptions; the upper ('Latin') half portrays the evangelists and has Latin scripts. The crown of the king of Hungary has superb stones like this one.

75 top left and right This gold coin-cum-seal dates from Sigismund's reign. It is inscribed with the name of the sovereign (right) and with that of his illustrious predecessor, Ladislas (left), crowned in 1077.

75 bottom left The early fourteenth-century coronation globe dates from the reign of Charles I. It is lined with gilded silver, has a double cross above and is decorated with the coats of arms of the Arpad and Angevin dynasties.

75 bottom right The rock crystal knob in the royal scepter is an Egyptian work from the tenth century. It features zoomorphic figures and elegant gold filigree representing the corollas of flowers. It can be seen in the Hungarian National Museum.

75 center right The imposing neo-classical entrance to the Hungarian National Museum is preceded by a limestone and bronze monument by Alajos Stròbl dedicated to Jànos Arany (1817-82), one of Petòfi's fellow independence fighters.

The most representative monument of the area is the Hungarian National Museum (Magyar Nemzeti Mùzeum). This neo-classical building (mid-nineteenth-century) has a façade on the lines of a Greek temple and stands in a garden decorated with statues of famous Hungarians of the past. The garden was the site where, on 15 March 1848, Sandor Petòfi declaimed his poem 'The National Song', which signaled the start of the war of independence against the Hapsburgs. The museum is where the Hungarian Crown Jewels are held, which were returned by the United States in 1978. These items include a golden globe, a crystal scepter, the magnificent coronation mantle and the famous crown used during the coronation of Stephen I that was sent as a gift by Pope Sylvester II; it is composed of a Byzantine diadem, a Latin diadem and a cross.

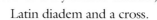

The Jewish quarter is found in Pest and has, in Dohàny Street, the largest synagogue in Europe. This was built in the second half of the nineteenth century in a composite style of Moorish and Byzantine elements. The synagogue also houses an interesting Jewish Museum that displays cult objects and documents relating to the history of the Jewish community. One of its most famous sons was Theodore Herzl, the man who founded Zionism. The second semi-circle inside the city is that of the Great Avenue (Nagyko'rùt), which is formed by five avenues that together measure a length of three miles. These were laid down in a city development plan at the end of the nineteenth century. These five avenues are always busy and very crowded at all hours of the day; they are not just the most popular shopping streets but are also lined by fine buildings. The most famous is the Museum of Applied Arts, at number 33, U'llo'i utca, the masterpiece of O'do'n Lechner, who was the inventor of what is known as 'the Hungarian style'. If the high, trapezoid roofs with colored tiles from the Zsolnay factory in Pécs and the central dome are western in concept, the interior is more like A Thousand and One Nights. The broad, white vestibule covered with iron and glass resembles the Alhambra in Granada but mixed with Indo-Iranian capitals and other decorative elements. And the museum collections, particularly those made by Zsolnay and the items of jewelry belonging to the Eszterhàzy treasure, are all of great interest. Another characteristic place in Pest is the New York Café (called Hungaria Café under the Communist regime), which is a traditional meeting place for intellectuals and artists. The spiral columns and mirrors inside are pure Art Nouveau. More decoration of the same epoch can be found in the old buffet in the West Station (Nyugati pàlyaudvar), which was built between 1874-77 by Gustav Eiffel's construction company. The trademark of the French engineer is seen in the perfect but daring iron and glass structure of the station. The most elegant street in the capital is Andràssy, which cuts across the Small and Great avenues and runs to Heroes' Square and the Park. The street is lined by eclectic apartment blocks and smart townhouses and emanates an atmosphere of Paris; this is not surprising as it was in 1858, at the time of the Austro-Hungarian monarchy and great city development projects, that the head of the government, Count Gyula Andràssy, returned from a trip to the French capital and decided to have this large arterial road built. The Opera House is nearly a copy of its sister theater in Vienna, built in neo-renaissance between 1875 and 1884 by Miklòs Ybl. The opulent decor of the façade is adorned by statues of 16 European composers, including the two Hungarians Franz Liszt and Franz Erkel, the latter being the composer of the national anthem. The frescoed and gilded interior is lined with wood and marble. Liszt's house-cum-museum can be visited in the nearby Vo'ro'smarty utca where he spent the last years of his life.

Andràssy Street opens into the city's most majestic square, Heroes' Square (Ho'so'k tere). Gazing down upon it are two important museums and the Millenary Monument, which was erected in 1896 to commemorate the conquest of the country by the Magyars. The monument is a tall column, on the top of which the Archangel Gabriel holds in one hand the crown of Saint Stephen; equestrian statues of the Arpad dynasty and six chiefs of Magyar tribes stand at the bottom. The tall column is ringed by a hemicycle colonnade; historical figures like Stephen I, Béla IV, Louis the Great, Matthias Corvinus and Lajos Kossuth (the hero of the 1848-49 revolution) are represented between the columns. The

('Portrait of Caterina Cornaro'). The large rooms of the museum also hold a wide range of Flemish and Dutch masterpieces, as well as works of German, Spanish, English and French painting. Masters such as Van Dyck, Vermeer, Rubens, Brueghel, Memling, Rembrandt, Durer, Holbein, Cranach the Elder, El Greco, Velasquez, Goya, Gainsborough, Constable, Hogarth, Poussin and Chardin are represented. The collection of modern art is also impressive, with works by Cézanne, Gauguin, Chagall and Kokoschka, as well as a number of Impressionists. The Arts Gallery, also housed in a building similar to a Greek temple, with a mosaic-lined façade, is usually used to accommodate temporary exhibitions.

78 The pediment of the Art Gallery in Heroes' Square is based on that of the Temple of Zeus in Olympia. Completed in 1906, this building was also constructed to celebrate the city's one thousandth anniversary.

78-79 The Millenary Monument in Heroes' Square commemorates the Magyars' conquest in 896 of the territory that is now Hungary. At the center of the colonnade, a column 118 feet high supports a statue of the Archangel Gabriel holding the crown and apostolic cross, symbols of the monarchy.

79 top left The impressive façade of the Fine Arts Museum was designed by Albert Schickedanz and Fulop Herzog in neoclassical style with a portico of eight columns. It houses the largest collection of figurative arts in the country.

79 top right The extraordinary 'Eszterhàzy Madonna' by Raphael was part of the art collection of the Eszterhàzy family. It was purchased by the state in 1870.

façade of the Fine Arts Museum has a portico with eight Corinthian columns and a pediment that is a copy of the one in the Temple of Zeus at Olympia. It displays fine collections of Egyptian, Greco-Roman, medieval and modern art. The Italian school is represented by Titian, Raphael (the famous 'Eszterhàzy Madonna'), Giorgione, Tiepolo and Bellini

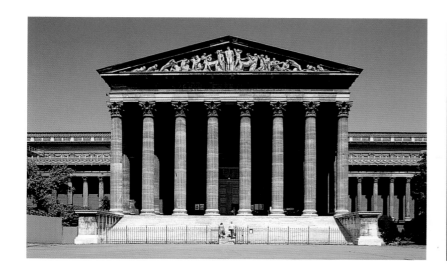

Lying next to Heroes' Square is the large City Park (Vàrosliget), almost a square mile in size, which was once a marsh and royal preserve. It is a place for walking through leafy avenues, taking boat rides on a small lake and for admiring architectural curiosities. On an island in the lake there is the fairy-tale, eclectic Vajdahunyad Castle, the design of which incorporates elements of Hungarian architecture, Segesvàr Castle (now Sighisoara in Rumania), and the Eszterhàzy residence near Sopron. The park is also where the Széchény Baths are located. Hot sulfurous water flows through its pools housed in a large neo-baroque building, crowned by a dome and adorned with statues of horses. Another extraordinary park in the Hungarian capital is Margaret Island (Margit-Sziget), which stretches for a mile and a half between Margaret and Arpad bridges. It was visited by the Romans who enjoyed the thermal springs there. It was used as a hunting reserve by the Arpad kings and was named after the daughter of Béla IV. At the time of the Mongol invasion, the king promised that when the country was liberated, he would consecrate his daughter Margaret (Margit) to God. The young girl was therefore closed in a convent whose ruins can be seen today. The large complex of the Palatinus Baths, with an open-air swimming pool, lies alongside the Danube opposite Buda in another testimony that Budapest, with over one hundred thermal springs, has been 'the city of the waters' since ancient times.

80 top left Vajdahunyad Castle is a blend of all Hungarian architectural styles, from Romanesque to Art Nouveau. The name comes from the Transylvanian castle belonging to the dynasty of Matthias Corvinus.

80 top right Margaret Island lies at the center of Budapest and is interesting for several reasons including the Palatinus complex with its thermal baths and the remains of the Dominican cloister and church where Margaret, the daughter of Béla IV, lived and died.

80-81 One of the attractions of the city park is the splendid Szécheny Baths in which the outdoor pool has water at a temperature near to 80°F and is surrounded by sculptural groups. Art Nouveau mosaics decorate the interior.

81 Chess can be played in the open-air pool in Széchény Baths even in winter. The temperature of the water in the central pool, 164 feet long, is above 80°F. The semicircular pools around it are even warmer.

82 top left In 1937, the highly original ceramicist Margit Kovàcs (1902-77) was awarded a diploma of honor at the World Fair in Paris. Her wonderful gothic figures – that are religious, mythological and popular in character and sometimes humorous – are now collected in a museum dedicated to her in an old merchant's house in Szentendre.

82 top right The city of Visegrad, situated in the heart of the Bend of the Danube, where the river rushes through a narrow gorge, was the residence of the king, Charles Robert, during the fourteenth century.

82-83 Eighteenth- and nineteenth-century buildings around Fötér are brightly painted and have curious wrought iron insignia. This is the main square in Szentendre, lined with art galleries and studios and dominated by the baroque Column of the Plague of 1763.

83 top right The main square in Szentendre sums up the romantic spirit of this town in the Bend of the Danube. Colored houses and churches of different confessions attract tourists interested to see a village typical of the past.

83 bottom right The special nature of Szentendre is the result of the meeting of the Serb and Hungarian cultures. At the end of the seventeenth century, many Serbs fleeing from the Turks formed a colony here that contributed strongly to the village, for example, by building the Orthodox Blagovestenska cathedral (1756-64), with its richly decorated iconostasis.

I n its course through Hungary, in addition to passing through Budapest, the Danube plays an important role in the area between the capital and Esztergom where it forms what is called the 'Bend of the Danube' (Duna-Kanyar). This is one of the most picturesque regions of the country, where natural beauty blends with historic remains. On the right bank of the river, the small town of Szentendre, which stands opposite the island of the same name, has been referred to as the 'Montmartre of Hungary' owing to its galleries and art museums (including that of the potter Margit Kovàcs), but the town's attractiveness lies above all in the harmoniousness of the huddle of 'toy houses' that lie around the Large Square (Fötér) and its 'Column of the Plague'. Pushing above the roofs of the houses are the bulb-shaped bell-towers of the churches, some of which (the Orthodox ones like the so-called 'Cathedral of Belgrade') were built by Serbs who, for various reasons over the centuries, settled in this idyllic village. A little to the north, framed by wooded hills, lies the extraordinary site chosen by the kings of Hungary for their residence: Visegrád. Originally the site of a Roman *castrum*, today it is a holiday destination for inhabitants of the capital. The ruins of the gothic and renaissance Royal Palace, which has partially been restored, date to the era of King Matthias who, with his wife Beatrice of Aragon, held a splendid court there. The Citadel was where the Crown Jewels were kept until 1440 when they were stolen by Elizabeth of Luxemburg to crown her son Ladislas V, though they were recovered some 20 years later.

The most important city on the Bend, Esztergom, which lies on a hill overlooking the Danube, was where it seems the Roman emperor Marcus Aurelius wrote part of his memoirs during the second half of the second century.

The capital of the Magyar kingdom from the eleventh to the thirteenth centuries, Slova Mansio is considered the seat of Catholicism in Hungary. Its most important monument is the neo-classical basilica completed in 1856 for the inauguration of which Franz Liszt wrote his 'Great Mass'. The treasures of the church are the sixteenth-century Bakòcz chapel – that was once part of the pre-existing cathedral of Saint Adalbert – and the collection of ecclesiastical jewelry. The greatness of Esztergom's past is apparent in what remains of the Royal Palace, which was destroyed by the Turks and since partly restored. The chapel has fourteenth-century frescoes and a rose window. In the palace, renaissance frescoes on the theme of virtue are attributed to Filippino Lippi's workshop.

Gyor lies almost on the Slovakian border. Of its four rivers, three flow into an arm of the Danube called the Moson. Originally a Celtic and Roman settlement, Gyor was fortified by Italian architects to withstand invasions and, in recent centuries, has become Hungary's largest industrial center. The elliptical Church of the Carmelites has an oval dome, an ele-

gant baroque façade and fine altarpieces painted by the Neapolitan artist, Martino Altomonte. Other religious buildings of value are the Church of Saint Ignatius, which was built on the model of the Church of Jesus in Rome, and the cathedral that stands on the top of a hill. Restyled on various occasions, the cathedral has a superb article in the gilded filigree reliquary of King Ladislas I, a masterpiece of medieval Hungarian craftsmanship.

96-97 Spacious Jurisics tér is lined by old houses, some of which contain the Crafts', Costume and Furniture museums.

97 top left Besides the medieval and baroque palaces that line three sides of the square, Jurisics tér boasts important religious buildings, like the baroque Szent Imre-templom dedicated to Saint Emericus, with a gothic apse, and the gothic Szent Jakab-templom.

97 top right The most important romanesque church in Hungary stands in the village of Jak. Consecrated in 1256 as part of a Benedictine monastery, the superb façade shows its Provencal and Norman influences. The nave and two aisles, supported by polystyle pillars, retains its fine thirteenth-century frescoes.

98 top Hungary's largest mosque stands in the central square of Pécs. It was built by Pasha Gazi Kassim around 1580 but was turned into a church after the Turks were chased out in 1686. The large cubic building is topped by an enormous dome crowned first by the Moslem crescent and later by the Christian cross to symbolize victory over Islam.

98-99 Pécs was originally a Celtic settlement and later inhabited by Frankish and Germanic tribes before the arrival of the Hungarians. In 1367 Louis the Great founded the country's first university here. The small, oval city center is a fascinating and harmonious blend of Turkish and Western styles.

99 top The memorial to the battle of Mohàcs fought in 1526 against the Turks is located close to Pécs. Over 100 carved wooden poles and a gate inscribed 'Here began the decline of a powerful Hungary' stand in a large grassy field where a ditch was dug to bury at least half of the 20,000 Magyars and Poles who died in the battle.

The most important city in Transdanubia is Pécs. It has an especially mild climate owing to its position on the south slopes of the Mecsek massif and still retains many buildings from the Ottoman epoch. Its history boasts the first university in Hungary (founded in 1367 by Louis the Great), the long presence of the Turks and the battle of Mohàcs, which was fought nearby in 1526.

The symbol of the city is the seventeenth-century mosque of Pasha Gazi Kassim, the most important Ottoman building in the country. Standing in the central Széchény Square, it was transformed into a church in the eighteenth century. The brick and stone building still has its original features, like decorative verses from the Koran and the *mihrab* that faces Mecca. The mosque of Pasha Hassan Jakovali is the only one not to have had its minaret destroyed, and it also houses an exhibition of Islamic art. Pécs can also boast Hungary's most famous ceramics factory: Zsolnay. An unusual fountain with four rams' heads in Széchény Square is made from that material. A handcrafts' museum exists close by in a picturesque house designed in a blend of styles.

The architecture of the Romanesque cathedral of Saint Peter is extraordinary to the eye. It has four towers, a nave and two aisles, a red marble renaissance altar, a painted coffered ceiling and walls decorated with geometrical patterns. Catacombs discovered beneath the parvis are

unique in central Europe for their enormous size and mosaic decorations.

Twenty-five miles outside of Pécs lie the memorial and park that commemorate the battle of Mohàcs. Carved poles in a vast meadow represent the troops and generals of the two armies – Hungarian and Turkish – and the dying horses.

99 bottom Of the thirteenth-century fortifications in Pécs only the barbican remains. This is a round rampart at the entrance to the city that, at one time, extended from the walls to the city gates. A public park now occupies that area.

Szigetvàr is a town dominated by an ancient fortress in whose courtyard there is another mosque that was transformed into a church. It too is related to an important historic event: the siege of the town was resisted for 33 days by Captain Miklòs Zrinyj in 1566 against a force of 90,000 Turks under Suleiman I, who died before the town was taken.

Its geographic position, warm shallow waters, attractive beaches and proximity to the capital (just 60 miles or so), makes Lake Balaton a favorite holiday resort of the inhabitants of Budapest but also of Hungarians in general. It became especially popular during the years when the Iron Curtain made leaving the country a difficult enterprise. The north shore is the most remarkable from a naturalistic standpoint and has an outstanding feature in the lovely Tihany Peninsula that extends a mile into the lake. Loved by poets and artists, this volcanic formation even has its own internal lake (Belso' tò) and is a delight for fishermen. The local Benedictine abbey was founded in 1055 by Andrew I, who lies buried in its crypt.

The main resort on the north shore is Balatonfu'red, which is famous for its curative waters that gush from five springs. These were developed into a spa during the eighteenth century and have been enjoyed ever since. The most original of these was built in exuberant Hungarian secession style and was named after the Empress Elisabeth. The gardens contain statues of some of the spa's most famous visitors, for example, Salvatore Quasimodo and Rabindranath Tagore, and the trees that these people planted.

The best vines in the grape-growing region around Balaton line the slopes of the basalt Badcsony Mountains that are volcanic in origin.

102 top Festetics castle has a superb park with rare species of trees hundreds of years old. In 1797 Count György Festetics founded Europe's first farming school (the Georgikon) here and organized poetry symposia that contributed to the reflowering of Magyar culture.

102 bottom Today the castle has a music school and several rooms reserved for conferences and receptions. The wife of one of the members of the family brought many original furnishings to Keszthely from England.

Farmhouses typical of the Hungarian countryside have high thatched roofs with exaggerated overhangs, and these are the main curiosity in the village of Szigliget. Not far away, in Keszthely, the visitor will find the largest baroque building in Transdanubia – the eighteenth-century castle that belonged to the Festetics family of landowners. The castle's magnificent Hélicon library contains tens of thousands of books and codices and is decorated with neo-classical furnishings. In Keszthely itself, it is worth visiting the gothic Franciscan church and the Balaton Museum for its archaeological and geological exhibits. Four miles out of the town, Lake Héviz is the largest hydrothermal lake in Europe at 10 acres in size, with sulfurous water at a warm 93°F.

102-103 In Festetics castle in Keszthely – the 'capital of Lake Balaton' – the Helikon Library boasts 90,000 books, illuminated manuscripts and incunabulae and a vast collection of writings about the lake. The collection belonged to Count György Festetics, an important individual during the Enlightenment.

103 right Construction of the castle began in 1745 but its current appearance is the result of the work done in 1883-87. Its 101 rooms are richly furnished and decorated with paintings by H. Robert and E. Adam and eighteenth- and nineteenth-century pottery.

104 top left The music school dedicated to the composer Zoltàn Kodàly (1882-1967) is an old monastery in Kecskemét. Kodàly's fame is owing to the attention he paid, with Béla Bartòk, to popular songs and folklore.

104 bottom left Kecskemét Town Hall was built between 1893-96; it was designed by Gyula Pàrtos and O'd'on Lechner, a master of the Hungarian secession style. It is lined with majolica tiles and has a magnificent wrought iron gate. Inside there are frescoes by Bertalan Székely in academic-romantic style.

104 right One of the most famous monuments in Kecskémet – the largest city in the Great Plain between the Danube and the Tisza – is the Cifra Palota or 'Grand House' built in 1902 in the style of the Hungarian secession style. The façade has colored decorations inspired by traditional ornamentation but also Islamic influences. It was designed by Géza Màrkus, a pupil of Lechner and was built using the polychrome majolica tiles from the Zsolnay factory in Pécs.

Veszprém perches on the hills and can boast the oldest bishopric in Hungary. Its bishop had the privilege of crowning the queens of Hungary, and, from the fourteenth century, also that of minting coins. The historic center of this ancient city is characterized by baroque architecture. Trinity Square is where the most important buildings stand: the Episcopal palace, the Giselle chapel (named after Stephen's wife who lived in Veszprém) and the Cathedral of Saint Michael, originally Romanesque, where the queens of Hungary were crowned and buried.

There is a fine view of the Bakony Mountains from the bottom of Var utca, the main street. When in Veszprém, it is worth making the side trip to Herend to visit the famous porcelain museum and see the delicate floral, leaf and butterfly designs.

The many pinewoods and sand dunes break the monotony of the flat countryside on Balaton's south shore. Popular in the summer for its lovely beaches, the largest resort on this shore is Siòfok, which has a port and the sailing center on the lake. Balatonmariafu'rdo', on the other hand, has a beach 6 miles long and a frescoed baroque church.

Kecskemét leads into the vast and intensively cultivated Great Plain where Hungary's agricultural traditions are to be seen. The name Kecskemét is linked to the production of apricots, so it is no surprise to find the famous *bàrackpàlinka* (apricot brandy) made here.

Two squares unite the most important buildings in the town. In Kossuth tér there is the baroque Franciscan church, the yellow and white Church of the Ascension and the eighteenth-century Calvinist temple with a split nave. The town hall was designed by O'do'n Lechner and Gyula Pàrtos and is an interesting example of Hungarian secession.

In the adjacent Szabadsàg tér stands the Great Synagogue built in Moorish style.

105 left
The magnificent town of Veszprém in the Transdanubia lies in the Bakony Mountains a few miles from Lake Balaton. The recently restored houses in its historic center are extremely picturesque. The town was the first bishopric in Hungary and its bishop had the privilege of crowning the queens.

105 top right
Perched on a hill, the castle district of Veszprém includes the gothic chapel of Giselle, one of the earliest medieval buildings in Hungary. A number of Italian military engineers were involved in the construction of the manor, for instance, Giulio Turco and Bernardo Gallo.

105 bottom right
Brightly colored facades and pediments line the pedestrian zone of Veszprém. The attraction of what was considered one of the loveliest cities in Transdanubia is also owing to the river Séd, which crosses it, creating many picturesque views.

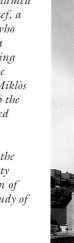

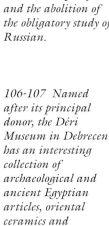

Szeged is a small town with a particularly mild climate that nestles in a gentle landscape of acacia trees. The town was completely rebuilt after being devastated by flooding of the river Tisza in 1879. Little remains of its history or of the fort built by Béla IV in 1242. The town's most important area is its magnificent central square that covers a full 12 acres and includes a park with allegorical statues. The architecture in the town is mainly neo-baroque with Austrian influences or eclectic, like the Town Hall.

Szeged's oldest building is the octagonal tower of Saint Demetrius in the Square of the Martyrs of Arad. Next to it stands the neo-Romanesque church built between 1915-30 to commemorate the flood. Inside, the church has Europe's second largest organ (after the cathedral in Milan) and a statue of the Virgin (patron saint of Hungary) in traditional costume.

Another monument that survived the flood is the Serbian church that has a lovely iconostasis and a rococo dome. The New Synagogue, built in 1900-03, is one of Europe's most renowned for its architecture and interior decoration.

The large town in the *puszta* of Hortobàgy, Debrecen, has been called the 'Calvinist Rome' as a Calvinist college was founded here in 1538 and Catholics were prohibited from practicing their religion in 1552. This background explains the dour appearance of the town, as exemplified by the Great

Calvinist Church, built in the early 1800s in neo-classical with ionic columns. It was in this church on 14 April 1849 that the Hungarian Parliament voted to depose the Hapsburgs.

The Reformed College is also in neo-classical, and close by in Déri tér (the square with four statues by sculptor Ferenc Medgyessy) there is the Frigyes Déri Museum, which has collections of paintings and cloaks worn by shepherds in the *puszta*.

Eger lies in the gentle, vine-covered hills that join the Bu'kk and Matra mountains in the northeast of Hungary. Famous for its Bulls Blood wine, the city's history is marked by a heroic episode that occurred in 1552. This was the siege of the town by 100,000 Turks that was victoriously resisted by 2,000 men, supported by their wives, and led by Istvàn Dobò, a legendary figure. All to no avail, however, as the Turks occupied the city just a few years later where they remained until 1687. The only vestige of that period is a minaret 135 feet tall. Naturally, the symbol of the city is the thirteenth-century fort that was destroyed in 1702 by Leopold Hapsburg so it would not fall into the hands of the fighters for independence. Though the fort is still under restoration, a network of underground tunnels has been discovered. The local history museum has interesting documents and Turkish objects from the collection of Bishop Giovanni Bekensloer, and the art gallery displays works by Hungarian, Austrian, Dutch and Italian painters. The city's epic moment is celebrated in Istvàn Dobò Square with a statue of the captain and a monument to the battle for the fort.

The Minorite church, with two towers, is dedicated to Saint Anthony of Padua. It was probably designed by the Austrian, Kilian Ignaz Dientzenhofer, and has a convex façade and a dome frescoed with a masterpiece of Hungarian baroque.

The neo-classical cathedral (the second largest in Hungary) has statues of four kings and saints by the Venetian Marco Casagrande and resembles a Greek temple with its Corinthian peristyle. Also in Liberty Square (Szabadsàg tér), the normal School in copf baroque has an eight-storey tower and houses an observatory and a museum of eighteenth-century instruments. The palace's library is frescoed and decorated with baroque oak furniture and is famous for its miniatures and volumes. The charm of Eger lies mainly in the city center where the little streets and gardens are lined with baroque buildings that hide elegant internal courtyards. One of the loveliest streets is Lajos Kossuth utca, where there are the remains of a Turkish bath and the eighteenth-century Committee Council building decorated with scenes from the Way of the Cross. Magnificent rococo frescoes by Henrik Fazola decorated the small palace in front of it.

117 top
The traditional clothing of the animal breeders in Hortobàgy puszta *is a wide-sleeved linen shirt, baggy trousers, boots and a wide-brimmed flat hat. Here the breeders show their riding skills.*

117 bottom
A typical scene from the puszta: *a cowboy follows his horses at the gallop on the endless grasslands of central Hungary.*

The *puszta* in Bugac is the kingdom of horseback shepherds, who watch over flocks of black and white sheep with long twisted horns. Hortobàgy National Park, to the west of Debrecen, has in its care the largest steppe in central Europe, an area that for centuries has provided grazing for flocks of sheep and herds of cattle and has resounded with the hooves of half-wild horses. When the rivers in the Great Plain were regulated – including the most important

tributary of the Danube, the Tisza, which rises in the Ukraine and is known as the 'blond river' for the sand it carries – the Hortobàgy was the only place remaining where traditional livestock raising methods were used. Today the Hortobàgy covers not only the puszta but the surrounding zones as well: these are the marshes with their unique flora and fauna and where migrating birds pause on their flights along the line of the Tisza.

118 top Farming in the Hungarian countryside is based on traditional methods. Farmers in Hortobàgy National Park transport their hay with animal-drawn carts.

118-119 A herd returns from the pasture under the watchful eye of the herder. In Hortobàgy National Park, horses, cattle and sheep are bred; animal breeding is Hungary's greatest economic resource.

119 top Equally common in Hortobàgy are flocks of white geese bred in large numbers. Their livers are used to produce Hungarian pâté, every bit as good as anything France can boast.

118 center A large flock of racka sheep in their enclosure on the puszta. *The scientific name of this curved horn breed is* Ovis stripeiceros hortobagyensis.

118 bottom The sturdy Hungarian gray ox is another characteristic animal of the puszta. *Their long horns are shaped like a lyre.*

120 top Badacsony is a range of modest truncated basalt hills in the middle of the most important wine-producing area of Balaton. This region produces excellent white wines.

120 center The solidified lava columns on the flanks of mounts Badacsony and Szentgyörgy are known as 'basalt organs'. They are surrounded by the lovely Olaszrizling vines, a yellowish-green Italian Riesling. Like many others, this vine was imported after the devastation caused by the phylloxera plant louse.

120 bottom Grape growing is very important to the Hungarian economy, though the surface area it covers has shrunk in recent years owing to an increase in both output and quality.

120-121 The ground beneath the vines around Lake Balaton is a reddish-violet color owing to minerals in the soil that make it very fertile. Wines from this zone are Raina rizling (Rhine Riesling), Tramini and the highly perfumed Zölszilvàni, which was originally from Transylvania.

121 top The climate of Lake Balaton is very salubrious: in the summer months the water of 'Hungary's sea' can reach 82°F though it cools if the sky is cloudy.

Transdanubia used to be the region called Pannonia by the Romans. It lies in the west of Hungary and covers an area of over 12,000 square miles between the Danube and the low mountains that, on the Austrian border, reach an average height of 2,000 feet. At the center of Pannonia lies Lake Balaton, the largest lake in central Europe (230 square miles); its size creates a microclimate that results in a particular flora and fauna and makes the lake appear like an inland sea. This large body of water in a country that has no coastline is also an expression of the feelings and expectations of the entire nation. Along the north shore of Lake Balaton, the pretty hills, about 1,100 feet in height, are volcanic in origin, so it is easy to find the ancient craters and thousands of stones that were thrown up by the eruptions. On the slopes of the Badacsony and Szentgyo'rgy hills stands the 'basalt organ', a series of columns of solidified lava that resemble the pipes of an organ. These formations are rooted in a soil rendered reddish violet by the mineral substances it contains and are surrounded by vineyards of contrasting colors as though painted on the landscape by Matisse. On the south side of the lake, the shore is flat with long strips of sand; the water is shallow and only gradually increases in depth. Little Balaton (Kis-Balaton) at the western tip of the large lake is an interesting area: 14 square miles of marsh are covered by lilies and rushes and provides a home to a vast population of waders, gulls, ducks and wild geese.

132-133 Around Pécs, in southern Hungary, the dance is for women only. In a sort of magical circle the women show off their foulards and brightly colored floral clothes over which they wear a white lace apron.

133 top The Tsigane (gypsy) dances at the horse festival in Hortobàgy National Park. The melodies of these people, who arrived in the Great Plain from India in the thirteenth and fourteenth centuries, can often be heard in restaurants and csárda.

INDEX

Note: c = *caption*

A

Adam, E., 103c
Adriatic Sea, 24, 87c
Alba Regia, 9
Albert Hapsburg, 28, 29
Alps, 131
Alsòvàros, 131
Altomonte, Martino, 84
America, 131
Andràssy, Gyula, 77
Andrew I, 100, 100c
Andrew II, the Jerusalemite, 24
Andrew III, 26
Anjou, 26, 74c
Anne of Chatillon, 54
Aquincum, 10, 22, 66, 66c
Aquitania, 23
Arany, Jànos, 75c
Arpad, 23, 24c, 26, 54, 74c, 78, 81
Asia, 9
Attila, 22
Augusta, 24
Austria, 34c, 36, 36c, 51, 87, 96c, 111c, 120, 123
Austrians, 12, 53, 65
Avars, 22

B

Baccio del Bianco, 84c
Badacsony Mountains, 100, 104, 105c, 120, 120c
Bakony forest, 10c
Balaton, lake, 9, 10c, 12c, 100, 100c, 104, 105c, 113, 113c, 120, 120c
Balatonfu'red, 100, 100c
Balcans, 27
Baltic Sea, 87
Bartok, Béla, 104c
Batu Khan, 26
Baumhorn, Lipòt, 107
Beatrice of Aragon, 31, 31c, 83
Bekensloer, Giovanni, 108
Béla III, 24, 54
Béla IV, 26, 26c, 54, 55, 61, 61c, 78, 81, 81c, 107
Belgrade, 29, 29c, 83
Bellini, 78
Benczùr, Gyula, 62
Bethlen, Istvan, 41
Black Sea, 22, 22c
Bo'rzso'ny Mountains, 123, 124
Bocksai, Ivan, 34
Bodrog, 10c, 111, 111c, 124, 124c
Bohemia, 28, 29c, 31, 34, 37c
Bonaparte, Napoleon, 84c
Bratislava, 9, 58c
Brueghel, 78
Bu'kk Mountains, 108, 124, 124c

Buda, 7c, 12, 12c, 26, 27, 28, 30c, 31, 33, 37c, 42, 42c, 43c, 53c, 55c, 61c, 63c, 65, 65c, 66c, 69, 70, 81, 84c
Budafok, 123
Budapest, 7c, 9, 10, 12, 12c, 22, 23, 33c, 36, 39c, 40c, 41, 41c, 42c, 43c, 45c, 46c, 47c, 49c, 50c, 53, 53c, 57c, 58, 58c, 62, 63c, 65, 65c, 73c, 81c, 83, 84c, 100, 122c, 123, 126
Bugac, 115c, 117
Bulgars, 23, 24c, 27c
Burgundy, 23
Byzantium, 54

C

Camicia, Cimenti, 30c
Carpathians, 22, 29c
Carrara, 70
Casagrande, Marco, 108, 109c
Ceresola, Venerio, 57c
Cézanne, Paul, 78
Chagall, Marc78
Chardin, Jean-Baptiste Simeon, 78
Charlemagne, 22
Charles I, 36, 40c, 74c
Charles III, 61, 72
Charles IV, 29c
Charles Robert of Anjou, 26, 27, 27c, 54, 55c, 83c
Charles V, 37c, 54
Clark, Adam, 53c
Claudius, 89
Coloman, the Bibliophile, 24
Comenius, 111
Constable, John, 78
Constance, Council of, 28
Constantinople, 24c
Contra Aquincum, 22, 65c
Corvinus, Matthias Valerius, 31
Corvinus, Matthias, 29c, 31, 31c, 54, 55, 58, 61, 61c, 62, 78, 81c, 83, 83c, 87
Cranach the Elder, 78
Croatia, 42c
Csàngòs, 12
Csepel, island of, 123
Cserhàt, 126
Czechia, 27
Czechoslovakia, 123

D

Danube, 9, 9c, 10, 12, 12c, 22, 22c, 26, 30c, 31, 42, 42c, 53, 53c, 57, 57c, 61, 61c, 65, 65c, 69, 70, 83, 83c, 84, 84c, 87, 104c, 113, 113c, 117, 120, 122c, 123, 123c, 129c
Debrecen, 12, 107, 107c
Dientzenhofer, Kilian Ignaz, 108

Diocletian, 22
Dnestr, 22
Dobò, Ferenc, 111
Dobò, Istvàn, 108, 108c, 109c
Don, 22
Dorfmeister, J., 89c
Dotis, 33c
Dòzsa, Gy'orgy, 33
Durer, Albrecht, 78

E

Eger, 108, 108c, 109c
Egyhàzaskeszo, 12
Eiffel, Gustav, 77
Eisenstadt, 89
El Greco, 78
Elisabeth of Luxemburg, 83
Elisabeth, 65, 100
England, 102c
Eravisci, 22c, 23c
Erkel, Ferenc, 77
Esterhàzy, Miklòs, 89c
Esztergom, 24, 83, 84, 84c, 122c, 123
Eugene of Savoy, 61, 72
Euphrates, 29c
Europe, 9, 12, 22, 24, 27, 28, 29, 30c, 51, 53, 61, 73c, 77, 81, 99, 100c, 107, 107c, 111, 115c, 117, 120, 123, 124

F

Fadrusz, Jànos, 61c
Fazola, Henrik, 108
Ferenc II Ràkòczi, 34
Ferenczy, Kàroly, 62
Ferö, lake, 89c
Fertod, 12c, 95c
Festetics, György, 102c, 103c
Feszl, Frigyes, 70c
Florence, 12
France, 34, 66
Francis I, 34, 58c
Franks, 22
Franz Josef I, 34c, 36, 37c, 54, 70c
Frederick Barbarossa, 24

G

Gainsborough, Thomas, 78
Ganz, 45c
Gauguin, Paul, 78
Gellert, Gerardo, 65c
Gellert, Mount, 12, 22c, 53c, 65, 65c
Geneva, 33c
Gepids, 22
Germany, 29c, 37c, 41, 42
Gerö, Ernö, 46c
Géza, 23, 24, 89
Giorgione, 78
Goya, Francisco José, 78
Granada, 77
Gresham, Thomas, 70c

Grundemann, Johann Basilius, 95c
Gyor, 47c, 84, 84c, 89, 124c

H

Hadik, Andràs, 57c
Hapsburg, 9, 12c, 26, 33, 34, 61, 75, 89, 107, 111, 111c
Hauszmann, Alajos, 69c
Haydn, Franz Josef, 12c, 89, 89c, 95c
Hegyalja, 124
Herend, 104
Herzl, Theodore, 77
Herzog, Fulop, 78c
Héviz, lake of, 100c
Hitler, Adolf, 42
Hogarth, William, 78
Holbein, Hans, 78
Hollòko, 126, 126c, 132c
Holt-Marcal, 124c
Holy Land, 24
Horn, Gyula, 51
Horthy, Miklòs, 40c, 41, 42, 45c, 107c
Hortobàgy, 117, 117c, 118c, 133c
Hungarians, 9, 22, 22c, 24c, 34c, 36, 99c, 100
Hungary, 7c, 9, 9c, 10, 10c, 12, 24, 26, 27, 27c, 29, 29c, 31, 33, 33c, 34, 34c, 36, 36c, 37c, 39c, 40c, 41, 42, 42c, 43c, 45, 47, 47c, 50c, 51, 53, 54, 58c, 65c, 69c, 70c, 74c, 77c, 83, 84, 84c, 87, 87c, 89c, 95c, 96, 97c, 99c, 104, 104c, 105c, 107, 107c, 108, 108c, 113, 115c, 117c, 118c, 120c, 123, 124, 131, 133c
Huns, 22
Hunyadi, Jànos, 28, 29, 29c, 31, 33, 58
Hus, Jan, 28, 29c
Hussites, 29

I

I'rottkö, Mount, 96c
India, 133c
Innocent XI, 58
Italy, 36, 41, 42

J

Jacoby, Miklòs, 89c
Jak, 97c
Jakovaly, Hassan, 99
Japan, 41
Jòkai, Mòr, 34c
Jollin, Gérard, 30c
Josef II
Jòszef, Attila, 107c
Juno, 23c
Jupiter, 23c
Jurisics, Miklòs, 96c

K

Kàdar, Jànos, 50c, 51
Kalocsà, 10c, 24, 63c, 131, 131c, 133c, 136c
Kàptalan, hill, 84c
Karlowitz, Peace of, 33
Karoly, Mihàly, 36, 37c, 39c, 69, 69c
Kassim, Gazi, 99, 99c
Kecskemét, 12, 43c, 104, 104c, 115c
Kékes, 124
Keszthely, 12c, 102, 102c, 103c
Khruschev, Nikita, 47
Kiskunsàg, 115
Kmetty, Janos, 39c
Ko'szeg, 96, 96c
Kodàly, Zoltàn, 104c
Koemloed, 23c
Kokoschka, Oskar, 78
Kossuth, Lajòs, 34, 34c, 69, 69c, 78, 107c
Kovàcs, Margit, 62, 83, 83c
Krafft, Pèter, 62
Kun, Béla, 36, 38c, 39c, 40c, 41c

L

Ladislas I, 24, 24c, 74c, 84, 109c
Ladislas II, 54
Ladislas V Hapsburg the Posthumous, 29
Ladislas V, 31, 83
Lajosmizse, 12c
Lamperth, Jozsef, 39c
Lantai, Lajos, 55c
Lechfeld, 24
Lechner, Ödön, 12c, 77, 104, 104c
Lenin, Vladimir, 45c, 47c
Leo VI the Philosopher, 23, 24c
Leopold Hapsburg, 108
Lippi, Filippino, 84
Liszt, Franz, 72c, 77, 77c, 84, 84c, 87
Little Balaton, 120
Loew, Emmanuel, 107c
Lombards, 22
London, 9, 70, 70c
Lorantffy, Zsuzsanna, 111c
Lotz, Kàroly, 55c, 69c
Louis I the Great, 27, 27c, 29c, 78, 99, 99c
Louis II Jagellon, 33, 33c

M

Magyars, 10, 22, 23, 24, 78, 109c
Mahomet II, 29c
Mahomet, 29c
Maléter, Pàl, 46c
Malinovskij, 43c
Marcus Aurelius, 84
Margaret Island, 12, 81, 81c
Maria Theresa, 34, 35c, 57c, 61, 62
Màrkus, Géza, 104c
Matisse, Henri, 120

Matra, 108, 124, 124c
Màtrahàza, 124
Mayerhoffer, 72
Mecca, 99
Mecsek massif, 99
Medgyessy, Ferenc, 107
Mediterranean Sea, 87
Mehmed II, 29
Melocco, Mikòs, 58c
Memling, Hans, 78
Merse Pal, Sziney, 63c
Mexico, 131
Milan, 107
Milldorfer, Josef Ignaz, 89
Mindszenty, Jòzsef, 45
Modena, 36
Mohàcs, 33, 99, 99c, 129, 129c
Mongols, 61c
Moravia, 31
Moson, 84
Muhi, 26
Munkàcsy, Mihàly, 62
Muslims, 131
Mustafa, Sokoli, 65c

N

Nagy, Imre, 45, 45c, 47, 50c, 51, 69, 69c
Nàndorfehérvàr, 29, 33
Naples, 23, 31c
New York, 50c, 77c
Nicola Giuseppe Eszterhàzy, 12c
Nicolas I, 34c
Nicopolis, 28, 29c

O

Obuda, 22, 53, 63c, 65, 66c
Olaszrizling, 120c
Orség, 131
Ostrogoths, 22
Otakar, 26c
Otto I the Great, 24
Ottomans, 10, 29c, 33c, 96c

P

Pàal, Làszlò, 62
Pannonhalma, 89
Pannonia, 10, 22, 23c, 120
Paris, 9, 12, 29c, 45, 83c
Pàrtos, Gyula, 104, 104c
Pécs, 12, 77, 99, 99c, 104c, 129, 133c
Pecz, Samu, 58c, 72c
Pest, 9c, 12, 26, 34, 34c, 43c, 53, 53c, 57, 57c, 63c, 65, 69, 69c, 70, 72c
Petofi, Sàndor, 34, 34c, 75c, 75c
Pogany, 39c
Poland, 26, 29c, 31, 33
Poussin, Nicolas, 78
Pozsony, 9, 33
Prussia, 36

Q

Quasimodo, Salvatore, 100

R

Raab, battle of, 84c

Ràba, 124c
Ràbca, 124c
Rajk, Laszlò, 44c, 45
Ràkòczi, Ferenc II, 69, 69c
Ràkòczi, György, 111c
Ràkosi, Matyas, 41c, 45, 45c, 46c, 47c
Rakovszky, 40c
Raphael, 78, 78c
Rembrandt, 78
Richard the Lionheart, 24
Richental, Ulric of, 29c
Rippl-Rònai, Jòszsef, 62
Robert, H., 103c
Romans, 10, 22, 28, 65, 81
Rome, 24, 84, 107
Rubens, Pierre Paul, 78
Rumania, 81

S

Saint Gerardo-Gellert, river, 65
Sàrospatak, 111, 111c
Saxons, 29c
Schedel, Hartmann, 30c
Schickedanz, Albert, 78c
Schulek, Frigyes, 55c, 57c
Scythians, 22c
Séd, river, 105c
Segesvàr, 34c, 81
Seine, 9
Serbs, 83, 83c
Sigismund of Luxemburg, 28, 29, 33, 54, 61, 74c
Siòfok, 104
Slavs, 22
Slesia, 31
Slovakia, 42c, 124c
Sopron, 12, 81, 87, 87c
Soroksàr, 123
Stalin, Joseph, 45c, 46c
Steindl, Imre, 69c
Stephen I, 10, 24, 25c, 37c, 57, 70c, 75, 78, 89, 104, 109c
Strauss, Johann, 53
Stròbl, Alajos, 37c, 57, 61c, 75c
Stuhlhoff, Sebestyén, 100c
Suleiman I, 33, 33c
Svatopluk, 22
Sylvester II, 10, 24
Szàlasi, 42
Széchényj, Ferenc, 62
Széchényj, Istvàn, 34
Szeged, 12, 22, 107, 107c, 131
Szekel, 29c
Székely, Bertalan, 55c, 104c
Székesfehérvar, 9
Szentendre, 9c, 83, 83c
Szentgyo'rgy, 120, 120c
Szigetvàr, 100
Szigetvàr, fortezza di, 33c
Szigliget, 102
Szombately, 96
Szrìnyi, Miklòs, 33c

T

Taban, 22c
Tabor, Janos, 39c

Tagore, Rabindranath, 100, 100c
Talbuchin, 43
Tàpiòszentmàrton, 22c
Teleki, Pàl, 42c
Temesvàr, 26
Thames, 9
Thwrocz, Johan de, 29c
Tiepolo, 78
Tihany penisula, 100, 100c
Tildy, Zoltàn, 45
Tisza, 9, 10, 10c, 104c, 107, 107c, 111c, 113, 113c, 124, 124c
Titian, 78
Tito, 44c
Tokay, 111, 111c, 124c
Torbagy, 40c
Transdanubia, 9, 23, 23c, 33c, 96c, 99, 102, 105c, 120, 129, 131
Transylvania, 28, 33, 34, 42, 81c, 111c, 120
Troger, Paul, 84c
Tuebingen, Hans von, 27c
Turks, 10, 28, 29, 29c, 31c, 33c, 34, 53, 55c, 61, 83c, 84, 84c, 96c, 99c, 100c, 108, 108c, 109c, 131

U

Ukraine, 117
Ungleich, Philippe, 57c
United States, 75
Urals, 10, 22
USSR, 42c, 45c, 47c

V

Vajk, 24
Van Dyck, Antonie, 78
Varga, Imre, 66, 66c
Varna, 29
Vasarely, Victor, 66
Velasquez, Diego, 78
Venice, 12, 24, 29
Vermeer, Jan, 78
Vészprem, 9c, 10c, 104, 105c
Vienna, 9, 34, 34c, 35c, 58c, 62, 78c, 96c
Viségrad, 9, 26, 31, 83, 83c, 123, 123c
Vìzivàros, 65, 84c
Vlaszlo I Jagellon, 29
Vlaszlo II Jagellon, 31
Vorosmarty, Mihàly, 61c, 70

W

Warsaw, 47
Weiss, 45c

Y

Ybl, Miklòs, 70c, 77
Yugoslavia, 42c

Z

Zeiller, Martin, 100
Zemplénihesyég, 124c
Zemplén-Tokay, 124
Zichi, Mihàly, 55c
Zrinyj, Miklòs, 100

136 The colorful apron worn by this woman in Kalocsà might be mistaken for a painting. Here, in the Great Plain, the most common handcraft is embroidery of women's clothing and household fabrics. At one time such fabrics were valuable presents for young peasant girls on their wedding day.